The Curious Incident of the Dog in the Night-time

A Complete Revision Guide for Edexcel IGCSE English Literature

Essential Literature: Complete Edexcel IGCSE Revision Series

Colour My Learning

BAILBROOK LANE

Written by Colour My Learning

© 2025 Xelium Ltd. All rights reserved.

Published by **Bailbrook Lane**, an imprint of Xelium Ltd.

Created in collaboration with **Colour My Learning**, a Xelium Ltd brand.

This product is for personal educational use only and may not be copied, redistributed, or modified without permission.

No part of this publication may be reproduced, stored in a retrieval system, or transmitted in any form or by any means electronic, mechanical, photocopying, recording, or otherwise without the prior written permission of the publisher, except in the case of brief quotations used for review or educational purposes. For licensing or permission enquiries, contact:

Bailbrook Lane info@bailbrooklane.com | www.bailbrooklane.com

In collaboration with: Colour My Learning www.colourmylearning.com

Cover design by Samuel JA Tan
Ebook ISBN: 978-1-913557-52-2
Paperback ISBN: 978-1-913557-53-9

Contents

Foreword	vii
1. INTRODUCTION	**1**
Purpose of This Guide	1
How to Use This Revision Guide	1
What's Inside and When to Use It:	2
Overview of the Exam Format (Edexcel IGCSE – Paper 2, 4ET1/02)	3
2. STORY OVERVIEW	**5**
Plot Summary	5
Brief Part-by-part Summaries	6
Part 1	6
Part 2	7
Detailed Part-by-Part Breakdown	8
Self-Test: Story Overview	12
3. MAIN CHARACTERS	**15**
Full Character List – *The Curious Incident of the Dog in the Night-time*	16
Detailed character profiles	18
Supporting Characters	36
Minor and Supporting Characters	44
Self-test: Main Characters	51
4. CONTEXTUAL BACKGROUND	**54**
Author Background and Purpose	55
Historical, Social, and Political Context	56
Theatre and Staging Influences	56
Thematic Relevance of Context	57
Structural and Symbolic Elements Supporting Context	59
Self-Test: Contextual Background	60

5. **MAIN THEMES AND KEY QUOTES** — 63
   - Honesty and Trust — 64
   - Family, Love, and Care — 67
   - Courage and Independence — 70
   - Loss and Grief — 72
   - Anger and Conflict — 74
   - Order and Chaos — 76
   - Adventure and Discovery — 79
   - How to Write About Themes in The Curious Incident of the Dog in the Night-time — 82
   - Self-Test Block: Main Themes — 84

6. **GLOSSARY OF KEY LITERARY AND DRAMATIC TERMS** — 87
   - Language Techniques — 88
   - Structure and Plot — 89
   - Dramatic Form and Devices — 91
   - Literary Concepts and Critical Terms — 92
   - Using This Glossary as You Write — 93
   - Self-test: Glossary of Literary and Dramatic Terms — 94

7. **LANGUAGE, FORM AND STRUCTURE** — 96
   - How to Use This Section — 97
   - Language — 97
   - Form — 102
   - Structure — 107
   - AO2 Starter Pack – Good Techniques to Learn First — 112
   - Self-test: Language, Form and Structure — 113

8. **HOW TO WRITE YOUR ESSAYS** — 115
   - Using a Structure to Plan and Write Effective Essays — 115
   - Sample Essay Plans — 120
   - Skeleton Structures for Essay Responses — 124
   - Why Use This Structure — 126
   - Planning Templates — 127

9. QUICK RECAP TOOLS	130
Revision Checklist	130
Fill-in-the-Blanks – Key Quotes	131
Multiple Choice Questions	132
10. PRACTICE QUESTIONS	135
Observed Trends	136
Revision Tips	136
Honesty and Trust	137
Family, Love, and Care	137
Courage and Independence	138
Loss and Grief	138
Anger and Conflict	139
Order and Chaos	140
Adventure and Discovery	140
Dramatic Form and Structure	141
Symbolism and Staging	141
Download: *The Curious Incident of the Dog in the Night-time* – Past Exam Questions by Theme (Ebook)	142
11. FURTHER READING AND RESOURCES	143
ColourMyLearning	144
BBC Bitesize – The Curious Incident of the Dog in the Night-time (play)	145
Edexcel Examiner Reports – English Literature Paper 2	145
Theatre and Production Insights	146
Contextual and Analytical Reading	147
ANSWER KEY	148
Chapter 2 Story Overview	148
Chapter 3 Main Characters	149
Chapter 4 Context	153
Chapter 5 Main Themes	155
Chapter 6 Glossary of Literary and Dramatic Terms	158
Chapter 7 Language Form and Structure	159
Chapter 9 Quick Recap Tools	161

Acknowledgments 163
Also by Colour My Learning 165

Foreword

Welcome to *The Curious Incident of the Dog in the Night-time* revision guide, created to support you as you work towards exam success and a deeper understanding of the play.

This guide is designed to complement, not replace, the teaching and guidance you receive from your teacher. Use it as a companion: to consolidate your learning, sharpen your analysis, and prepare effectively for your English Literature exam.

Every effort has been made to ensure the content is accurate, useful, and aligned with the Edexcel IGCSE specification. If you notice any errors or have suggestions for improvement, we would be grateful to hear from you. Your feedback helps us make future editions even better.

If you find this guide helpful, we'd love to hear from you. You can leave a review on: Amazon or Bailbrook Lane

We wish you every success in your studies. Read critically,

Foreword

revise actively and write with clarity and purpose. Good luck in your exams!

With best wishes,

The team at **Colour My Learning**

and **Bailbrook Lane**

Chapter 1
Introduction

Purpose of This Guide

This guide is designed to help you if you are studying *The Curious Incident of the Dog in the Night-time* for the Edexcel International GCSE in English Literature prepare effectively for the exam. It focuses on helping you:

- understand key characters, themes, and context
- analyse language, structure and form
- practise applying their knowledge to exam-style questions

How to Use This Revision Guide

This guide is designed to support your study of *The Curious Incident of the Dog in the Night-time* **after you've completed your first reading of the play** whether in class or independently. It provides a clear structure to help you revise plot, explore themes, understand characters, and prepare effectively for your exam.

Use it as a complete revision tool or return to specific sections as needed.

What's Inside and When to Use It:

1. **Start with the Story Overview** Begin by revisiting the plot summary and key turning points. This helps you anchor your understanding of what happens — and why it matters.
2. **Study the Characters and Themes Together** Each theme is explored alongside key character contributions and carefully selected quotes with analysis. This combined approach helps you understand how Priestley uses character to communicate ideas and build meaning.
3. **Revisit Language, Form and Structure** This section helps you meet AO2 by explaining how the play is constructed and how specific techniques affect the audience. Use the model paragraphs as a reference when planning your own essays.
4. **Apply What You've Learned** You'll find past paper questions, short tasks, and planning prompts that allow you to put your knowledge into practice. Use these for timed practice, homework, or in-class activities.
5. **Review Key Quotes and Ideas** Quick-recap tools and quote summaries are included throughout, so you can revise efficiently and reinforce what you've learned.

This guide can be used alongside classroom teaching or for independent revision. Whether you're working steadily across the term or reviewing ahead of your exams, it offers structured support to help you write clearly, revise with focus, and understand the play with confidence.

Overview of the Exam Format (Edexcel IGCSE – Paper 2, 4ET1/02)

Section A: Modern Drama

This section accounts for 20% of the total English Literature Qualification.

- 1 hour 30 minutes total paper (including Section B: Literary Heritage)
- Choose 1 out of 2 questions on The Curious Incident of the Dog in the Night-time
- 30 marks | Spend approx. 45 minutes
- Open book: You may take a clean copy of the play into the exam

You are expected to

- demonstrate a close understanding of their drama text
- maintain a critical style
- present an informed personal engagement
- understand how writers create literary effects
- understand and use appropriate literary terminology
- identify and use relevant examples from the play.

The Curious Incident of the Dog in the Night-time

Assessment Objectives Tested:

AO1: Understanding of the text and personal engagement (15 marks)

AO2: Analysis of language, form, and structure (15 marks)

Chapter 2
Story Overview

Plot Summary

The Curious Incident of the Dog in the Night-time, adapted by Simon Stephens from Mark Haddon's novel, is a modern bildungsroman that follows **Christopher Boone**, a 15-year-old boy from Swindon who interprets the world through logic, mathematics and precision.

One evening, he discovers Wellington, his neighbour's dog, lying dead with a garden fork in its side. Determined to uncover the culprit, Christopher begins a detective mission that leads to unexpected discoveries about his own family.

Through his investigation, Christopher finds out that his father, Ed, lied about his mother's death and killed Wellington in a fit of rage. Christopher decides to leave Swindon for London to find Judy, his mother. Along the way he faces enormous challenges, strange places, large crowds, loud noises, which the play conveys through striking staging and physical theatre.

In the end, Christopher reunites with his mother, excels in his A-level Maths exam, and begins to rebuild fragile trust with his father. His journey turns out to be more than solving Wellington's murder. It is also about finding independence and proving to himself that he is capable of extraordinary things.

✏ Quick Check: In one sentence, explain how Christopher's journey is about more than solving Wellington's murder.

Brief Part-by-part Summaries

Part 1

- The play begins with Christopher discovering Wellington's body in Mrs Shears's garden.
- Questioned by the police, Christopher decides to act as a detective, recording everything in a book which his teacher, Siobhan, reads aloud on stage.
- His investigation reveals tensions between his father Ed, his absent mother Judy, and the Shears family.
- Despite Ed's warnings, Christopher questions neighbours and discovers hidden letters from Judy, proving she is alive and living in London.
- In a heated confrontation, Ed admits he lied about Judy's death and also confesses that he killed Wellington.

✏️ **Extension Task:** Part 1 is a series of short scenes where Christopher and Siobhan often "share" the storytelling. How does this structure help the audience see the world through Christopher's perspective?

Part 2

- Feeling unsafe with Ed, Christopher makes the brave decision to travel alone to London to find Judy.
- His journey through the train station, underground, and London streets is overwhelming, shown on stage with sound, movement, and projections to reflect sensory overload.
- Christopher finds Judy living with Roger Shears. She is shocked but glad to see him, and tries to comfort him despite her messy personal life.
- Ed arrives and tries to regain Christopher's trust, but Christopher cannot forgive him.
- Christopher takes his A-level Maths exam and achieves top marks, proving his mathematical ability and determination.
- The play closes with Christopher asking "Does that mean I can do anything?"

For additional practice and to understand the plot better:

AO1: In a couple of sentences, explain how Part 1 sets up Christopher's investigation and leads to the revelation about his father.

AO2: Explain how *sound and projected text* is used, in Part 2 to represent Christopher's experience of the underground.

Detailed Part-by-Part Breakdown

Part 1: Mystery, Discovery and Betrayal (Scenes 1-27)

Scene 1: Wellington's Death

The play begins dramatically in Mrs Shears's garden. Wellington, her dog, lies dead with a garden fork sticking out of him. Christopher kneels beside the dog, touches it, and lifts its paw. Mrs Shears screams when she sees him, and the police arrive. When a policeman touches Christopher, he panics and hits him. This misunderstanding leads to his arrest.

Scenes 2-8: Becoming the Detective

After being released, Christopher decides to investigate Wellington's death. With encouragement from Siobhan, his teacher, he begins writing everything down in a book. On stage, Siobhan reads from the book, so the audience can follow Christopher's story from his perspective and directly through his words. He questions neighbours about the night of Wellington's death. He is determined to investigate what he believes to be a crime. His father, Ed, becomes angry and warns him to stay out of other people's business.

Scenes 9-16: Clues and Ambitions

As Christopher continues to collect information, he also explains his love of maths and space, his dislike of metaphors, and his ambition to take an A-level in Maths. Mrs Alexander, a kindly neighbour, shares some unexpected information: Christopher's mother, Judy, (whom he believes is dead) had an affair with Mr Shears.

Scenes 17–23: Conflict at Home

Ed discovers Christopher's book and is furious when he learns that Christopher is still investigating Wellington's death. He confiscates the book and hides it. Their relationship becomes increasingly tense.

Scenes 24–26: The Hidden Letters

While looking for his book in his father's bedroom, Christopher accidentally finds a box of unopened envelopes addressed to him. Inside are letters written by Judy, his mother, dated after the time Ed told him she had died. On stage, Judy and Siobhan (reading) take turns to narrate the letter's contents.

Scene 27: Ed's Confession

When confronted, Ed breaks down and admits he lied to Christopher. He explains that Judy left home. In his desperation, Ed also confesses that he killed Wellington in a fit of anger after Eileen (Mrs Shears) rejected him. For Christopher, the logic is simple and terrifying: if Father lied about Mother, and if Father could kill a dog, then he might kill him too. Christopher's trust in Ed is destroyed and he decides that he has to leave home.

🖉 **Extension Task:** Write a short diary entry (120 words) as Christopher, immediately after discovering the letters. Describe how you feel about Father and Mother.

Part 2: Flight, Overload, and Fragile Repair (Scenes 28–57)

Scene 28: School: Staging a Play

Siobhan and Mrs Gascoyne want to stage a play of Christopher's story. But he refuses. Meanwhile, Ed is looking for Christopher.

Scenes 29–35: Swindon Station

Christopher plans carefully. He takes Ed's bank card and remembers the four-digit PIN. At the station, he buys a ticket and waits for the train. The environment is noisy and overwhelming, with announcements, signs, and crowds all around him. The play often uses overlapping voices and fast transitions here, reflecting how confusing the station feels for Christopher. His logical problem-solving skills, like remembering maps and instructions, help him cope. A policeman finds him and tries to get him to return home to Ed, but the train starts moving. Christopher hides from the policeman and arrives in London.

Scenes 36–38: The Underground Journey

Christopher struggles with escalators and the crowded platforms. At one point he drops his pet rat, Toby, onto the tracks. In a tense moment, he climbs down to rescue Toby and manages to get back onto the platform just before a train arrives. Eventually, he boards the Tube train to Willesden.

Scenes 39–41: Judy's Flat

Christopher waits for Judy and Roger outside their flat. She is shocked but delighted to see him. Judy explains that she left Ed to live with Roger Shears, but she admits she has not been a good mother. Roger, however, is annoyed and does not want Christopher there.

Scenes 42–47: Family Tensions

Ed arrives in London, desperate to make peace, but Christopher will not go near him. Judy tries to calm the situation, but the tension between all three adults is clear. Roger's frustration is clear, and Judy begins to see that her choices are damaging Christopher.

Scenes 48–54: Returning Home

Judy moves back to Swindon with Christopher in time for Christopher to sit his A-level exam. Christopher sits his A-level Maths exam despite being very tired and hungry. Ed tells Christopher that he is proud of him.

Scenes 55–56: New home

Christopher and Judy move to their own place. Christopher visits Ed's house every day but still does not trust him. Eventually, Ed buys Christopher a puppy, which Christopher names Sandy. Ed is determined to regain Christopher's trust.

The Curious Incident of the Dog in the Night-time

Scene 57: Closing Moment

In the final scene, Christopher receives his exam results. He looks back at everything he has accomplished: solving Wellington's murder, uncovering the truth about his parents, travelling to London alone, reuniting with his mother, and passing his exam. He asks, "Does that mean I can do anything?" The play ends without answering this question directly, leaving the audience with both hope for Christopher's future and awareness of the challenges that still lie ahead for Christopher.

✏ **Extension Task:** Imagine you are Christopher, writing the final entry in your "murder mystery" book. In about 120 words, sum up what you achieved and how you feel about your future.

Self-Test: Story Overview

Use the following questions to check your understanding. No peeking — test yourself from memory first.

Multiple Choice:

1. Where does Christopher discover Wellington's body?
    a. In Judy's garden
    b. In Mrs Shears's garden
    c. In Mr Shears's garage
    d. In Siobhan's classroom

2. Why is Christopher arrested at the start of the play?
   a. He is caught trespassing in Mrs Alexander's garden
   b. He is accused of killing Wellington
   c. He hits a policeman who touches him
   d. He refuses to answer police questions
3. Which neighbour tells Christopher about Judy's affair with Roger Shears?
   a. Mrs Alexander
   b. Mrs Shears
   c. Ed Boone
   d. Siobhan
4. What important discovery does Christopher make in Ed's bedroom?
   a. Wellington's body
   b. Judy's clothes
   c. A box of letters from Judy
   d. Roger Shears hiding

Short Answers:

5. Why does Ed tell Christopher that Judy is dead, and how does Christopher find out the truth?
6. What decision does Christopher make after Ed's confession, and why is it so significant?
7. How does Judy react when Christopher arrives at her flat in Willesden?

The Curious Incident of the Dog in the Night-time

Longer Task

8. In your own words, explain how the two parts of the play show Christopher's growth. Write one paragraph based on each Part of the play.

Chapter 3
Main Characters

In *The Curious Incident of the Dog in the Night-time*, Simon Stephens adapts Mark Haddon's novel into a play that places Christopher Boone at the centre of every event. Around him, different characters play crucial roles in shaping the mystery, the family conflict, and contributing to Christopher's journey towards independence.

This section explores the significance of each character within the play. You will find:

- a full list of characters grouped into main, offstage, and minor figures
- detailed profiles that reveal key traits and motivations
- how each character changes (or refuses to change) as the story progresses
- their role in Christopher's growth and challenges
- links to major themes such as truth, family, bravery, and trust
- key moments and quotes to support exam responses

Understanding these characters in depth is crucial to mastering AO1 and AO2, demonstrating close knowledge of the text and analysing how the characters represent and create meaning.

Exam questions often ask about **how a character is presented** (such as Siobhan's trustworthiness or Ed's responsibilities as a father), or about a **theme shown through a character** (such as bravery, loss, or independence). As you read these profiles, think about what the characters do, and also how their actions and words are used to complement and expand Christopher's world.

Full Character List – *The Curious Incident of the Dog in the Night-time*

Main Characters

1. **Christopher Boone** – Fifteen-year-old protagonist, gifted at maths, determined to uncover the truth.
2. **Ed Boone** – Christopher's father, protective but secretive, struggles with anger.
3. **Judy Boone** – Christopher's mother, leaves to live with Roger Shears in London.
4. **Siobhan** – Christopher's teacher, supportive and understanding.

On-Stage Supporting Characters

1. **Mrs Alexander** – Elderly neighbour, kind to Christopher, reveals Judy's affair.
2. **Mrs Shears** – Neighbour and owner of Wellington; her dog's death sparks the investigation and she clashes with both Christopher and Ed.
3. **Roger Shears** – Judy's partner in London, previously married to Mrs Shears.

Minor and Supporting Characters

- **Mrs Gascoyne** – Headteacher at Christopher's school
- **Reverend Peters** – Reverend at Christopher's school
- **Policemen** – Represent authority and appear in key confrontations.
- **Station Guards and Strangers** – Appear during Christopher's journey to London.
- **Ensemble Voices** – Actors who double roles to create the wider world on stage.

✏️ Quick Recap: Group the characters into three categories: Main, Supporting, and Minor. Write one sentence on why each group is important to the play's structure.

Detailed character profiles

Main Characters

Christopher Boone

Role in Plot:

Christopher is the 15-year-old protagonist and narrator of the play. The entire story is shaped through his perspective, often spoken directly to the audience or read from his book by his teacher, Siobhan. His investigation into Wellington's death begins as a detective puzzle but grows into a journey of independence and self-discovery. Christopher's role drives the narrative, but it also shapes the play's unique form: his voice and logic dictate how the audience experiences his world on stage.

Key Traits:

Logical, mathematically gifted, determined, honest, struggles with metaphors and social conventions, highly observant, brave in his own way.

Motivations:

Initially, Christopher is motivated by a simple goal: to solve the mystery of Wellington's death and write it all down in his book. His drive for truth and his need for routine and logic keep him focused, even when his father wants him to stop.

After he discovers Judy's letters and hears Ed's confessions, his motivation changes. He no longer feels safe at home and decides that he needs to see Judy in London. His purpose eventually changes again. Scoring an A+ for his A-level Maths exam and caring for Toby and Sandy become his ways of proving that he can be independent and capable.

Character Development:

Early on, Christopher depends on routine and adult support, particularly from Ed and Siobhan. His investigation forces him outside these routines, gradually building his independence and resilience. The train journey to London is the turning point where he confronts fear and chaos independently.

After Christopher achieves his goal of sitting the A-level Maths exam, he asks, *"Does that mean I can do anything?"* His development is both practical (travelling alone) and symbolic (believing in his own ability and potential).

Symbolism:

Christopher symbolises logic, truth, and the desire for order. His precise way of speaking and narrating gives the play its distinctive structure. He also symbolises resilience: his ability to confront fears (crowds, travel, confrontation) reflects the theme of courage and bravery. Christopher's book, that Siobhan reads aloud, represents his need to be heard and understood on his own terms.

Themes Linked:

Honesty and Trust, Family, Love and Care, Courage and Independence, Adventure and Discovery

Key Moments / Turning Points:

- **Scene 1**: Discovers Wellington's body and is wrongly accused by police.
- **Scene 8**: Begins writing his book, framing the play.

- **Scene 18-19**: Learns from Mrs Alexander about Judy and Roger's affair.
- **Scene 12:** Clashes with Ed over the investigation, introducing the theme of truth and lies.
- **Scene 23-24:** Finds Judy's letters, realising she is alive and that Ed has lied to him. It is a pivotal discovery that reshapes the family story.
- **Scene 27**: Loses trust in Ed after his confession about Wellington.
- **Scene 32-38**: Travels alone to London, confronting overwhelming fear and sensory overload and rescues Toby from the train tracks.
- **Scene 56**: Ed gives Christopher a puppy and works to rebuild their relationship.
- **Scene 57**: Scores highly in his A-level Maths exam. Ends by asking, *"Does that mean I can do anything?"*
- After the play, Christopher stays to present to the remaining audience his mathematical proof.

Conflicts & Interactions:

- **With Ed:** Their relationship embodies the theme of truth and lies. Ed's secrecy and temper clash with Christopher's demand for total honesty, creating the play's central conflict.
- **With Judy:** Initially shaped by her absence, their relationship is rebuilt when Christopher goes to London. Christopher's literal honesty challenges Judy's guilt but also allows her a chance for redemption.
- **With Siobhan:** She is his trusted guide and often the voice that offers security. Their calm, supportive

interaction contrasts with the volatility of his relationship with his parents
- **With the Audience:** Christopher frequently addresses the audience directly (breaking the fourth wall), pulling them into his logical perspective. Dramatically, this interaction makes the audience experience the world as he does.

Quotes (with Analysis):

"My name is Christopher John Francis Boone. I know all the countries of the world and capital cities. And every prime number to 7,507."
His precise self-introduction highlights his logical, factual way of thinking and immediately defines his distinctive narrative voice.

"I do not tell lies."
Summarises Christopher's moral code; his honesty forms the play's central contrast with adult deception.

"I find people confusing."
Reveals his difficulty interpreting social cues and connects directly to the play's exploration of communication and misunderstanding.

"I see everything."
A simple statement that explains Christopher's extraordinary attention to detail, which drives both his detective skills and his sensory overload.

The Curious Incident of the Dog in the Night-time

"Father had killed Wellington who is a dog so that meant that he could kill me."
Expresses his logical fear and the complete loss of trust in his father after his confession.

"I found my mother. I was brave."
Marks his growing independence and resilience. Courage for him means facing chaos logically.

"Does that mean I can do anything?"
Ends the play with uncertainty and hope, suggesting both progress and self-doubt. Christopher acknowledges his progress yet is also aware of the limits of his new confidence.

✏️ Extension Task: Write a short paragraph (100–120 words) from Christopher's perspective, explaining why you always tell the truth. Use an example from the play to show how telling the truth shapes what happens to you.

✏️ Discuss: Christopher's motivations change as the play develops from solving Wellington's death to becoming independent. Which stage of his journey do you think shows the most courage, and why?

Ed Boone

Role in Plot:

Ed is Christopher's father and main carer at the start of the play. He works to provide stability for his son but makes very questionable choices — lying about Judy's death and killing Wellington — that create the play's central conflict. His actions and eventual confession drives Christopher's investigation, his journey to London, and ultimately his need for greater independence. Ed's role challenges the audience to think about the limits of love, trust, and responsibility in family life.

Key Traits:

Protective, practical, short-tempered, secretive, loving but flawed, proud, emotionally volatile.

Motivations:

Ed's motivations are layered and sometimes contradictory:

- **Protection:** He claims he lied about Judy's death to protect Christopher.
- **Anger:** Ed's frustration at Christopher's inflexibility and single-mindedness often manifests in anger. This climaxes when he hits Christopher.
- **Resentment:** Judy's departure left him bitter and abandoned, which likely influenced his decision to cut her out of Christopher's life.
- **Pride / Emasculation:** Losing Judy to Roger Shears humiliated him, and lying about her may have been a way of regaining control.

- **Revenge / Control:** Hiding Judy's letters and declaring her "dead" can also be read as an act of revenge and an attempt to dominate the family narrative.

These complex layers show Ed as a flawed but caring figure whose love is tinged with anger and self-pride.

Character Development:

Ed's role changes after Christopher discovers the letters and his confession about Wellington. From then on, he becomes desperate to regain his son's trust. By the end, although their relationship is still strained, Ed shows his love by respecting Christopher's boundaries and presenting him with a puppy.

Symbolism:

Ed represents the challenges of parenting under pressure. His actions show both the strength of parental love and the damage caused when trust is broken.

Themes Linked:

Honesty and Trust, Family and Relationships, Love, Care and Attachment, Loss and Grief, Anger and Conflict, Order and Chaos.

Key Moments / Turning Points:

- **Scene 4:** Defends Christopher after his arrest, presenting himself as protective and responsible.
- **Scene 6:** Orders Christopher to stop investigating Wellington; shows his temper and irritation.
- **Scene 25-26:** Christopher finds Judy's letters, exposing Ed's deception.
- **Scene 27:** Admits to lying about Judy and confesses to killing Wellington — the dramatic climax of Act 1.
- **Scene 55:** Attempts to rebuild trust with Christopher by giving him a puppy, symbolising reconciliation.

Conflicts & Interactions:

- **With Christopher:** Their relationship is the heart of the play. Ed's lies about Judy and Wellington destroy trust, forcing Christopher towards independence. Dramatically, their conflict embodies the theme of truth and lies.
- **With Judy:** Their failed marriage reveals deeper issues — arguments, resentment, and differing parenting styles. Judy's absence and Ed's anger fuel his choices.
- **With Mrs Shears:** Their strained connection reflects Ed's loneliness and need for support, but also his volatility.
- **With Himself:** Ed's pride and anger conflict with his love for Christopher, creating an inner struggle that drives the play's tension.

The Curious Incident of the Dog in the Night-time

Quotes (with Analysis):

"I cooked his meals. I cleaned his clothes. I looked after him every weekend."
Reflects Ed's pride in his role as a single parent and his frustration at the pressure of constant responsibility. The list of actions emphasises his reliability and emotional fatigue.

"Just try and keep your nose out of other people's business."
Reveals his quick temper and defensive nature. The command implies a need to control the situation and conceal the truth from Christopher.

"The truth is so hard to tell sometimes."
Suggests that his lies come from fear rather than cruelty. It captures the play's tension between honesty, protection, and emotional pain.

"I killed Wellington, Christopher."
This blunt admission is the play's turning point, completely destroying the trust between father and son.

"Christopher, I would never, ever do anything to hurt you."
Expresses his desperate need for forgiveness. "Never ever" underlines both his sincerity and the irony of his past actions.

"You have to know that I am going to tell you the truth from now on."
Conveys his attempt to rebuild trust through honesty. The phrase "from now on" admits past failure while promising change.

"You have to learn to trust me."
Reveals his need for reconciliation but also the imbalance in their relationship; trust must now be earned rather than expected.

"I've got you a puppy."
A quiet gesture of love and repair. The puppy becomes a symbol of loyalty and new beginnings between father and son.

✎ Quick Recap: List three ways Ed tries to protect Christopher. For each, explain whether it helps or harms their relationship.

The Curious Incident of the Dog in the Night-time

Judy Boone

Role in Plot:

Judy is Christopher's mother. At first, Christopher believes she has died of a heart attack, he learns the truth when he discovers the letters she wrote from London. Judy left Ed for Roger Shears because she felt trapped, frustrated, and unable to cope with Christopher's needs. Her reappearance in Part 2 shifts the direction of the play, forcing Christopher to reassess his family and giving the audience a more complex picture of parental love.

Key Traits:

Emotional, impulsive, protective, insecure. loving but inconsistent, guilt-ridden, caring, determined to make amends.

Motivations:

- Judy wants to escape the constant stress and conflict of her marriage.
- She feels overwhelmed by the pressures of parenting Christopher.
- She longs for affection and validation, which she finds in her relationship with Roger.
- Her guilt motivates her to write letters and explain her actions.
- When reunited with Christopher, she works to rebuild trust, provide reassurance and comfort.

Character Development:

At the start, Judy is "absent", defined by Ed's lie that she has died. Through the letters, her voice emerges: honest, regretful, and emotionally raw. These letters complicate the audience's view of her as a flawed but loving mother. When Christopher finds her in London, Judy's warmth and protection, is a contrast to Ed's anger. By the end, she plays a more active role in Christopher's life, supporting him through his exam and providing him reassurance, encouraging him to rebuild his relationship with his father.

Symbolism:

Judy represents the difficulties of being a parent to a special-needs child especially when a marriage is also strained. She also symbolises both the fragility and resilience of family relationships as her absence highlights themes of loss and broken families. The letters reveal her hidden truth and her attempt to reach out across distance and time. Judy's return represents the possibility of reconciliation, even when relationships have been damaged.

Themes Linked:

Honesty and , Family and Relationships, Love, Care and Attachment, Loss and Grief, Anger and Conflict.

Key Moments / Turning Points:

- **Scene 23-24:** Christopher discovers Judy's letters in Ed's room, learning she is alive.
- **Scene 39:** Christopher arrives at Judy's London flat; she is surprised but takes him in.

- **Scene 40-43:** Judy stands up for Christopher and protects him.
- **Scene 49:** Judy takes Christopher back to Swindon.
- **Scene 52:** She takes Christopher to his exam and meets Siobhan.

Conflicts & Interactions:

- **With Ed:** Their marriage broke down under the pressure of arguments, resentment, and conflicting approaches to parenting.
- **With Christopher:** Judy feels guilt for leaving him, but their reunion allows her to rebuild a bond with honesty and care.
- **With Herself:** She struggles with regret and feelings of inadequacy as a mother.
- **With Roger:** Their relationship highlights Judy's search for happiness, but it also highlights her instability.

Quotes (with Analysis):

"Dear Christopher, I was looking through some old photos last night..." (from her letter)
Conveys her warmth and nostalgia. The direct, conversational tone maintains emotional connection despite distance.

"I was not a very good mother, Christopher."
Expresses guilt and self-awareness, revealing Judy's honesty about her failings.

"It broke my heart but eventually I decided it would be better for all of us if I went."
Reveals her inner conflict. She sees leaving as an act of love, even though it caused pain.

"Bloody Nora, it's cold!"
Brings Judy to life in Christopher's memory through natural, colloquial speech.

"Christopher, it's OK. There aren't any sharks. Touch my hand."
Reflects her instinctive care and calm reassurance, using touch to bridge emotional distance.

"I won't let him hurt you. You're safe with me."
Demonstrates her protective nature and her determination to reassert her role as Christopher's guardian.

"It's only an exam. You can take it again."
Although misplaced, her attempt to comfort Christopher emphasises her empathy and patience. This contrasts her gentler approach with Ed's more rigid expectations.

✎ Extension Task: "Judy is presented as both loving and flawed in her role as a mother." How far do you agree? Write an essay plan, include at least three quotations.

The Curious Incident of the Dog in the Night-time

Siobhan

Role in Plot:

Siobhan is Christopher's teacher, mentor, and the play's narrator. She reads aloud from his book and clarifies his thoughts, guiding both Christopher and the audience.

Within the story, she represents stability and encouragement, offering him a safe space to express himself and be understood.

Key Traits:

Supportive, patient, calm, understanding, trustworthy, encouraging, insightful, a consistent mediator between Christopher and audience.

Motivations:

Siobhan is motivated by her role as an educator. She wants Christopher to express himself with confidence and to be understood. Her reading from his book serves both a personal and dramatic purpose, ensuring his voice is heard and his logic made accessible to others. Her encouragement demonstrates how empathy and education can empower independence.

Character Development:

Siobhan is presented as a constant presence rather than a changing character. Her stability contrasts with Ed and Judy's volatility, explaining why Christopher trusts her. As he grows more independent, she remains the steady voice guiding both him and the audience. Her closing narration reinforces Christopher's development and her continuing role as the bridge between his private world and public understanding.

Symbolism:

Siobhan symbolises trust, empathy, and communication. She embodies how consistency and understanding create stability in Christopher's chaotic world. As narrator, she is the bridge between his purely logical way of understanding and the audience's need for emotional clarity, reinforcing her dual role as teacher and interpreter.

Themes Linked:

Honesty and Trust, Love, Care and Attachment, Order and Chaos

Key Moments / Turning Points:

- **Scene 1:** Reads from Christopher's book, establishing her dual role as teacher and narrator.
- **Scene 5-8:** Interacts calmly with Christopher, her narration encourages empathy and understanding from the audience.
- **Scene 17:** Advises Christopher to listen to his father, balancing empathy with practicality.
- **Scene 20:** Helps him process emotions surrounding his parents' actions and understand the concept of lying.
- **Scene 28:** Transforms Christopher's book into the play the audience is watching, reinforcing her framing role.
- **Scene 55:** Acts as a sounding board while setting clear emotional and professional boundaries.

- **Scene 57:** Hands Christopher his A-level results, closing the play with affirmation and stability.

Conflicts & Interactions:

- **With Christopher:** A trusted mentor whose calm support contrasts with Ed and Judy's volatility. Her consistent guidance enables Christopher to thrive and communicate with confidence.
- **With the Audience:** As narrator, she translates Christopher's thoughts and feelings, shaping audience understanding with empathy rather than judgement.
- **Within the Play's Structure:** Siobhan faces no personal conflict; her consistency is a deliberate dramatic device, providing stability in a story built on tension and uncertainty.

Quotes (with Analysis):

"It was seven minutes after midnight. The dog was lying on the grass in the middle of the lawn in front of Mrs Shears's house."
Siobhan opens the play by reading from Christopher's book. Her calm narration introduces the meta-theatrical structure. The play we see is literally Christopher's written account voiced through her.

"This is good, Christopher. It's quite exciting. The details make it more realistic."
Reflects her supportive, guiding role. She helps him shape his writing and gives him confidence while modelling clarity and observation.

"If your father said you have to stop, then I think he probably has a good reason and you should stop. But you can still be very proud because what you've written so far is great."
Balances empathy and authority. Siobhan respects Ed's wishes while affirming Christopher's achievement, embodying the emotional stability he depends on.

"Not all murders are solved. Not all murderers are caught."
Offers perspective and closure, teaching Christopher to accept uncertainty. It is an idea that mirrors the play's larger moral ambiguity.

"Christopher, I want to ask you something. Mrs Gascoyne wondered if we would like to do a play this year."
Encourages him to share his story with others, encouraging trust and growth. Siobhan becomes both teacher and collaborator, helping his private voice reach a public audience.

"It's your result. You need to open it and read it."
Keeps him in control of his success. Her calm instruction affirms his independence as he achieves his A* and takes ownership of his learning.

"Oh. Oh, That's just. That's terrific."
Her unguarded joy captures the pride and affection she feels as a teacher; it's one of the play's few moments of uncomplicated warmth.

"You were [brave]."
The final affirmation before the play's closing question. Siobhan's reassurance anchors the ending, linking courage with self-belief and reinforcing her role as moral compass.

🖊 Reflection Task: Why is Siobhan such an important character in the play? Write three reasons, using evidence from her interactions with Christopher.

🖊 Discuss Task: How far do you agree that Siobhan represents stability in Christopher's life? Use at least two quotations to support your view.

Supporting Characters

Mrs Alexander

Role in Plot:

Mrs Alexander is Christopher's elderly neighbour. She is kind and patient with him, and she plays an important role in the investigation by revealing Judy's affair with Roger Shears. Her honesty suggests that truth, even when painful, can be an act of care. She represents understanding from outside the family and highlights how small acts of kindness can make a difference.

Key Traits:

Kind, patient, inquisitive, trustworthy, observant.

Motivations:

Mrs Alexander's motivation is simple kindness. She reaches out to Christopher with warmth and genuine concern, offering biscuits and companionship. Her decision to tell Christopher about Judy and Roger reflects her belief that honesty matters, even when it causes pain.

Character Development:

Mrs Alexander remains consistent throughout the play. Her steadiness contrasts with Ed and Judy's flaws, which makes her reliability stand out and explains why Christopher responds to her kindness.

Symbolism:

Mrs Alexander symbolises kindness, honesty, and community. Her warmth contrasts with Mrs Shears's defensiveness and Ed's secrecy. Her openness brings both comfort and disruption, suggesting that compassion can coexist with painful truth.

Themes Linked:

Honesty and Truth, Family and Relationships, Anger and Conflict.

Key Moments / Turning Points:

- Offers Christopher biscuits and tries to connect with him.
- Reveals Judy's affair with Roger Shears. This is a turning point that shatters Ed's version of the truth and pushes Christopher to question everything he has been told.

- Provides a calm and caring presence in contrast to the chaos of Christopher's family life.

Conflicts & Interactions:

- **With Christopher**: She is initially a source of comfort and encouragement, but also the person who tells him the truth about Judy and Roger — a revelation that devastates him even as it brings him closer to the truth.
- **With the Plot:** Her decision to tell the truth provides Christopher with essential information, driving the narrative forward.

Quotes (with Analysis):

"Do you want to come in for some biscuits?"
A simple, genuine offer that conveys warmth and social openness. Her kindness and patience contrast with the tension within Christopher's family.

"Your mother... your mother was very good friends with Mr Shears."
The pause and euphemism reveal her sensitivity and restraint. Although she intends compassion, this moment exposes the affair that destabilises Christopher's world and propels the investigation forward.

"I think you are very brave."
Expresses gentle admiration and emotional intelligence. Her reassurance validates Christopher's courage and reinforces her role as a quiet moral presence.

Mrs (Eileen) Shears

Role in Plot:

Mrs Shears is the Boones' neighbour and Wellington the dog's owner. She appears in the opening scenes when Christopher discovers her dead dog. It is this event that sets the entire play in motion. Her anger triggers the central mystery and exposes the tension within both the family and community life.

Her kindness to Ed after Judy leaves, is misinterpreted as something more, as Ed sought comfort and companionship beyond a neighbourly relationship. When these feeling are not reciprocated, it reinforces his sense of loss and isolation.

Key Traits:

Practical, blunt, quick-tempered, defensive, emotionally-strained.

Motivations:

Mrs Shears initially offers support to Ed after Judy leaves, but her behaviour is shaped by conflicting emotions. Having been betrayed by her husband Roger and hurt by Judy, she feels both sympathy and resentment.

There are hints that Ed's connection with Mrs Shears extends beyond simple friendship. While the play never confirms an affair, his dependence on her after Judy leaves and his later anger imply unspoken emotional needs and rejection. This adds depth to Ed's loneliness and helps explain his loss of control when Wellington is killed.

Character Development:

Mrs Shears does not undergo significant change. She functions mainly as a catalyst: Wellington's death sparks the investigation, and her clashes with Christopher and Ed expose a deeper conflict within the community.

Symbolism:

Mrs Shears symbolises the outside world's limited understanding and tolerance. She embodies the theme of community under strain, where neighbours offer brief support yet also contribute to tension and isolation

Themes Linked:

Honesty and Trust, Family and Relationships, Loss and Grief, Anger and Conflict

Key Moments / Turning Points:

- **Scene 1:** Christopher finds Wellington in her garden; she accuses him.
- **Scene 10:** Threatens to call the police when Christopher visits her.

Conflicts & Interactions:

- **With Ed**: Their relationship, once briefly supportive, becomes strained when she distances herself. The implication that Ed wanted more than friendship explains part of his anger and isolation later in the play.

- **With Christopher**: Her lack of patience may reflect the emotional strain she feels, making her harsher towards him than other adults like Siobhan or Mrs Alexander.

Quotes (with Analysis):

"What the hell were you doing in my garden?"
Aggressive tone establishes conflict from the opening scene and sets up the central mystery.

"Get away from my bloody dog!"
Emotional outburst conveys both grief and defensiveness, revealing the intensity of her reaction and frustration towards Christopher.

✏️ Quick Recap: Why might Mrs Shears feel both sympathy and resentment towards Ed and Christopher? Give one reason for each, based on the events of the play.

Roger Shears

Role in Plot:

Roger is Judy's partner in London and Mrs Shears's former husband. Although he appears only briefly on stage, his presence shapes the family conflict: Judy leaves Ed for him, fuelling Ed's resentment and deception. Roger's unreliability later isolates Judy, affecting her ability to care for Christopher.

The Curious Incident of the Dog in the Night-time

Key Traits:

Self-centred, unreliable, evasive, emotionally-detached.

Motivations:

Roger seeks companionship without responsibility. He takes Judy in, but when life with Christopher proves demanding, he retreats. His near-total absence on stage reflects his emotional avoidance and lack of commitment.

Character Development:

Roger does not develop on stage, but others' references to him change how we view the Boone family. At first, he represents escape and excitement for Judy. Later, his failure to provide stability exposes her regret and reinforces her disillusionment in trying to find a stable romantic relationship.

Symbolism:

Roger symbolises betrayal, instability, and irresponsibility. For Ed, he embodies humiliation and rivalry; for Judy, he represents the illusion of escape that turns hollow. His absence becomes a metaphor for emotional neglect and the fragility of adult relationships.

Themes Linked:

Family Breakdown, Love and Betrayal, Responsibility, Independence.

Key Moments / Turning Points:

- Mentioned by Mrs Alexander, whose revelation of Judy's affair with him exposes the hidden fractures within the Boone family.

- Reappears in Judy's letters as the man she left Ed for, revealing both her desire for freedom and her guilt.
- His eventual withdrawal from Judy underscores her vulnerability and the emptiness of her escape.

Conflicts & Interactions:

- **With Judy (reported):** Offers affection and a sense of adventure at first but ultimately abandons her, exposing her emotional instability and dependence.
- **With Ed (indirect):** The affair ignites Ed's resentment and pride, motivating his lies about Judy's death.
- **With Christopher (indirect):** Roger's presence and actions fractures Christopher's world, making him central to the emotional turmoil despite never meeting him.

Quotes (with Analysis):

"What the hell is going on?"
Roger's opening line when he discovers Christopher in their flat. His abrupt language and disbelief establish him immediately as hostile and unwelcoming.

"Jumping Jack Christ."
A sarcastic outburst that conveys exasperation and disdain. The blasphemous expression exposes his coarse, impatient nature and emotional volatility.

"What's he going to do? There's no school for him to go to. We've both got jobs. It's bloody ridiculous."
The string of rhetorical questions turns Judy's problem into an

inconvenience. His frustration and self-interest reveal his focus on practicality over compassion.

"A gold star, Well that's very original I have to say."
Mocking tone diminishes Judy's attempts to help Christopher. The sarcasm underscores Roger's lack of empathy and emotional immaturity, leaving Judy and Christopher isolated.

"You think you're so clever, don't you? Don't you ever think about other people for one second, eh? Well I bet you're really pleased with yourself now aren't you?
Bitter accusation that exposes Roger's hypocrisy and insecurity. His misplaced anger contrasts sharply with Christopher's innocence and highlights his irresponsibility.

✏️ Extension Task: Why is Roger Shears important to the story, even though he rarely appears on stage? Write two short paragraphs using evidence from the play.

Minor and Supporting Characters

- **Mrs Gascoyne** – Headteacher at Christopher's school
- **Reverend Peters** – Reverend at Christopher's school
- **Policemen** – Represent authority and appear in key confrontations.
- **Station Guards and Strangers** – Appear during Christopher's journey to London.
- **Ensemble Voices** – Actors who double roles to create the wider world on stage.

Although *The Curious Incident of the Dog in the Night-time* focuses mainly on Christopher and his family, several minor characters help to build the world around him. Figures such as Mrs Gascoyne, Reverend Peters, the policemen, and the strangers at the station reveal how different people respond to Christopher — with patience, confusion, or frustration. These smaller roles add realism, shape the play's tone, and highlight key themes such as communication, authority, and understanding. The ensemble voices, who play multiple roles, also help the audience experience the world as Christopher does: fast-moving, noisy, and sometimes overwhelming.

Mrs Gascoyne

Role in Plot:

Mrs Gascoyne is the headteacher of Christopher's school. She appears in short but crucial scenes that show the limitations of institutional support. Her reluctance to let Christopher take the A-level exam demonstrates how systems underestimate him, while her eventual agreement signals small but meaningful progress.

Key Traits:

Authoritative, cautious, bureaucratic, pragmatic.

Motivations:

Mrs Gascoyne, as Headteacher is all about rules and responsibility. She wants to protect Christopher and the school from failure, but her caution initially limits his opportunity to achieve more.

Character Development:

Though her role is brief, she shifts from doubt to acceptance, allowing Christopher to sit the A-level. Her change reflects how understanding can grow when others learn to see beyond labels.

Symbolism:

Mrs Gascoyne symbolises institutional barriers and the slow pace of change. She represents how systems often fail to recognise individual potential until it is proven.

Related Themes:

Education, Support, Independence, Perception, Achievement.

Key Moments / Turning Points:

- **Scene 14:** Debates with Ed about how Christopher cannot be allowed to take the exam.
- **Scene 28**: Tries to convince Christopher to let his book be turned in to a play.

Quotes (with Analysis):

"I can't treat Christopher differently to any other student."
Reflects the cautious language of institutional limitation. Her formal tone highlights the barriers Christopher faces within education.

"It would set a precedent."
She is worried about breaking rules or giving special treatment. Her focus on procedure represents how schools can sometimes hold students back instead of helping them.

"I think it could be really fun."
A rare moment of warmth from Mrs Gascoyne. Her lighter tone shows she can be encouraging, hinting that she is beginning to see Christopher's creativity in a new way.

Reverend Peters

Role in Plot:

Reverend Peters is a priest at Christopher's school who appears in the classroom scenes and as the invigilator during Christopher's A-level Maths exam. He represents authority and politeness but struggles to understand Christopher's literal thinking. His presence brings moments of light humour and highlights the communication gap between Christopher and the adult world.

Key Traits:

Well-meaning, conventional, polite, easily flustered, limited in understanding.

Motivations:

Reverend Peters wants to be supportive but operates within social and religious norms that Christopher questions. His attempts at comfort, such as explaining Heaven, expose his lack of insight into Christopher's logical worldview.

Symbolism:

He symbolises formal religion and polite society. Adults who mean well but cannot fully comprehend Christopher's perception of truth. His character critiques superficial empathy and the limits of conventional reassurance.

Related Themes:

Faith and Logic, Communication, Understanding Others, Authority.

Key Moments / Turning Points:

Scene 11: Classroom scene: Christopher tries to discuss the location of Heaven, revealing the clash between faith and logic.

Scene 53: invigilates Christopher's Maths exam, highlighting Christopher's determination to do well in his exam despite recent challenging circumstances.

Quotes (with Analysis):

"I suppose what it really means is that they are with God."
A kind but vague answer that Christopher finds confusing. It shows how adults prefer to offer emotional comfort instead of clear, logical explanations.

"Turn over the paper please Christopher. And begin."
His steady presence during the exam complements Christopher's growing confidence and independence.

Policemen

The policemen represent **authority, rules, and misunderstanding**. When Christopher hits the first policeman, it is clear how easily he is misread by those who do not understand him. Their short, direct lines and uniforms create tension and realism on stage. They show how official systems respond harshly to deviations from order and discipline rather than with empathy.

Key moments:

- **Scene 2** – The Policeman questions Christopher and arrests him after he reacts to being touched.
- **Scene 33 & 34b** – The Station Policeman acts on Ed's report of Christopher missing. He catches up with Christopher on a train.
- **Scene 41** – The London Policeman speaks to Christopher at Judy's home to confirm that he is safe to stay with her.

Station Guards and Strangers

These background figures appear during Christopher's journey to London. They represent the **confusing and unpredictable outside world**. Their rushed dialogue and overlapping voices on stage create a sense of noise and overload. Most treat Christopher with impatience, though some offer brief help. They represent how society often struggles to make space for people who think differently.

Key moment:

Scene 32-35 – Christopher navigates the train station and Underground, surrounded by fast-moving strangers and guards shouting instructions.

Ensemble Voices

The ensemble voices are **actors who double multiple roles**, creating a shifting, dynamic world around Christopher. This technique helps the audience experience the story through Christopher's perspective.

The same actors appear as teachers, neighbours, and strangers, blurring boundaries between safe and unsafe spaces. Their collective presence also reminds the audience that Christopher's story is surrounded by systems, institutions, and expectations.

Key function: Reflect Christopher's sensory experience, movement, sound, and overlapping dialogue express his confusion and isolation.

Together, these minor and supporting characters bring depth and realism to Christopher's world, helping us see how he interacts with, but is often misunderstood by the people around him.

Self-test: Main Characters

Multiple Choice Questions

Choose the best answer for each question.

1. Which character first reveals to Christopher that Judy had an affair with Roger Shears?
   a. Siobhan
   b. Mrs Shears
   c. Mrs Alexander
   d. A Policeman
2. Why does Ed tell Christopher that Judy is dead?
   a. To protect Christopher from grief
   b. To punish Judy
   c. To avoid admitting the truth about her leaving
   d. All of the above
3. What motivates Judy to write letters to Christopher?
   a. She wants to confuse him
   b. She feels guilty and wants to explain herself
   c. Ed asked her to
   d. She wants to hide the truth about Roger
4. Which character acts as the narrator of the play, reading aloud from Christopher's book?
   a. Ed Boone
   b. Siobhan
   c. Judy Boone
   d. Mrs Alexander

The Curious Incident of the Dog in the Night-time

1. What role does Wellington's death play in the plot?
    a. It shows Ed's anger
    b. It begins Christopher's investigation
    c. It reveals Roger's betrayal
    d. It causes Judy to return

Short Answer Questions

Write 1–2 sentence responses.

2. What does Christopher mean when he says, "I always tell the truth"?
3. How do Ed's lies about Judy affect his relationship with Christopher?
4. What does Judy's line, "I was not a very good mother, Christopher," reveal about her self-perception?
5. How does Siobhan act as a bridge between Christopher and the audience?

Longer Tasks

Character & Theme Connection

6. Choose one main character (Christopher, Ed, or Judy). Explain how that character explores the theme of *Family and Relationships*. Include:
    - A brief summary of the character's role in the play
    - At least one quotation how truth or lies affect them
    - A comment on how language or staging is used to present this theme

Compare & Contrast

7. How do Judy and Ed differ in their love and support for Christopher? Consider:
    - Their honesty and trustworthiness
    - Their choices and emotional responses
    - How their behaviour shapes Christopher's relationship with each of them

Character Symbolism

8. What does Wellington's death represent in the play? Why is it important that this is the starting point of the story? Include:
    - How it sets the detective structure in motion
    - How it symbolises secrecy, anger, and mistrust
    - How it shapes the audience's understanding of Christopher's struggles and perspectives

Supporting Characters

9. Choose either Mrs Alexander, Mrs Shears, or Roger Shears. Explain how this character to reveals something important about Christopher's world. Consider:
    - Their relationship or influence on Christopher
    - How they connect to the themes of honesty, trust, or family conflict
    - Why their role matters even if they are less central to the play

Chapter 4
Contextual Background

A note on Context and the Exam

It is important to note that context is not directly assessed in Section A of Edexcel IGCSE English Literature Paper 2. The assessment criteria for this section focus solely on:

- **AO1**: Demonstrating detailed knowledge and understanding of the text, while presenting a critical and personally engaged response.
- **AO2**: Analysing the writer's use of language, form, and structure to create meaning and achieve effects.

However, a clear understanding of historical, social, and the writer's context will help you support stronger interpretations of the play, particularly when analysing character motivations, thematic development, or dramatic structure. Context should always be used in support of AO1 or AO2, rather than as standalone factual information.

Author Background and Purpose

When Mark Haddon wrote the novel *The Curious Incident of the Dog in the Night-time* in 2003, It quickly became a bestseller, praised for its unique narrative voice. Haddon wrote on his blog that *"The Curious Incident* is not a book about Asperger's ... if anything it's a novel about difference, about being an outsider, about seeing the world in a surprising and revealing way". The novel invites readers to understand Christopher's mind on its own terms.

Simon Stephens' Adaptation

Playwright Simon Stephens adapted the novel for the stage in 2012. His purpose was to honour the clarity of Christopher's voice while transforming the story into a theatrical event. Stephens worked with director Marianne Elliott and the theatre company Frantic Assembly to use movement, projections, and sound to show Christopher's inner world. The play is a theatrical exploration of perception, truth, and resilience.

Siobhan's Role

In the play, Siobhan (Christopher's teacher) performs a structural role as she guides the audience through Christopher's story, reading from his book and helping to shape how we understand his thoughts. Siobhan becomes a bridge between Christopher and the audience: his voice is filtered through her supportive presence, ensuring that the audience never loses sight of his humanity and logic.

✏️ Reflection: How does knowing Haddon did not intend the novel to be "about autism" change how we interpret Christopher's story?

✏️ Discuss: How does Siobhan help both Christopher and the audience connect to the story?

Historical, Social, and Political Context

Britain in the Early 2000s

- Growing awareness of autism and neurodiversity, but also misunderstanding and stigma.
- Increasing family breakdown and divorce, reflected in Christopher's fractured family situation.
- Changing social attitudes toward disability and inclusion, with more discussion of special educational needs in schools.
- A backdrop of ordinary suburban life — trains, schools, small communities — against which Christopher's extraordinary way of seeing the world stands out.

Theatre and Staging Influences

- National Theatre premiere (2012): a landmark production, transferring to the West End and Broadway.
- Frantic Assembly's movement direction created the physical storytelling style: lifts, ensemble work, and visual metaphors for Christopher's thinking.
- Use of projections, grids, and lighting to represent logic, maths, and sensory overload.

- Theatre became a way to immerse the audience in Christopher's perspective

✏ Quick Recap: Name one social issue in early 2000s Britain that influences the play.

✏ Extension Task: How might awareness of autism and inclusion in education shape how audiences respond to Christopher's character?

Thematic Relevance of Context

Although context is not assessed independently, it underpins many of the play's central themes. When considered alongside analysis of language, form, and structure, it helps explain why Stephens made particular choices in adapting the novel for the stage and how these choices resonate with audiences.

Honesty and Communication

In early 2000s Britain, ideas about openness, honesty, and communication were becoming central to public and family life. This is reflected through Christopher's insistence on truth and his struggle to understand adult lies. His literal way of speaking challenges a society that often hides behind politeness or avoidance.

Trust and Independence

The play was written during a time of growing awareness of inclusion and independence for young people with additional needs. Christopher's journey to London mirrors these real social debates. His ability to navigate the world alone becomes both a personal triumph and a symbol of changing attitudes toward autonomy and trust.

Courage and Resilience

Christopher's courage to face noise, travel, and uncertainty reflects everyday resilience for those who see or experience the world differently. In a culture that often underestimates neurodiverse individuals, his quiet courage redefines what strength looks like.

Family and Relationships

The rise in divorce and family separation in early 2000s Britain shapes the play's portrait of the Boone family. The play explores what family means when traditional structures fail, focusing on care, loyalty, and the effort it takes to rebuild damaged connections.

Love, Care, and Attachment

Judy, Ed, and Siobhan each express love differently, through emotion, protection, or encouragement. Their contrasts reflect a society becoming more aware of emotional literacy and the importance of showing care in ways others can recognise and accept.

Loss and Anger

Loss and anger appear in both family breakdown and everyday frustration. Personal emotion is linked with wider social themes, grief, guilt, and the pressure of modern life, revealing how love and pain coexist in families under strain.

Order and Chaos

The early 2000s saw rapid social change and technological growth. The play's grid-like staging, mathematical motifs, and moments of sensory overload echo the tension between control and chaos in modern life. Christopher's need for logic becomes a way to find order in a confusing world.

Adventure and Discovery

Christopher's detective journey connects to a long British storytelling tradition of quest and adventure. Yet his "adventure" takes place in familiar, urban spaces, trains, stations, homes, reminding audiences that discovery can happen in everyday life when people learn to face fear with courage.

🖊 Quick Recap: How does understanding the social and cultural context of early 2000s Britain help explain the play's focus on honesty, independence, and resilience?

🖊 Reflection: How does Christopher's determination to be independent link to broader social discussions about disability rights?

Structural and Symbolic Elements Supporting Context

1. **Prime numbers**: Christopher derives comfort and security from narrating and repeating ordered numbers.
2. **The book within a play:** Christopher's writing becomes a play we are watching, a self-conscious reminder of perspective and storytelling.

3. **The stage as a grid/black box:** evokes both mathematical precision and the sense of Christopher's mind.
4. **Ensemble staging:** ordinary settings (a train, a street) transform through physical theatre, showing the world as Christopher perceives it.

🖉 Quick Recap: Why are prime numbers used to order Christopher's chapters?

🖉 Discuss: How do projections, grids, or ensemble movement help the audience step inside Christopher's perspective?

Understanding the social and theatrical context behind *The Curious Incident of the Dog in the Night-time* helps explain how the performance, structure, and language are used to explore the play's main themes.

Self-Test: Contextual Background

Do keep in mind that context is not directly examined in this part of the exam. We have included it here to enrich your understanding of the play and Simon Stephens' intentions in adapting it. You can test your understanding of the historical, social, and theatrical context that shapes *The Curious Incident of the Dog in the Night-time*.

Colour My Learning

Multiple Choice Questions

1. Who adapted Mark Haddon's novel *The Curious Incident of the Dog in the Night-time* into a stage play?
   a. Marianne Elliott
   b. Simon Stephens
   c. Scott Graham
   d. Ed Boone
2. In the play, which character reads Christopher's writing aloud to guide the audience?
   a. Judy
   b. Siobhan
   c. Mrs Shears
   d. Roger Shears
3. Which theatre company developed the physical staging style used in the play?
   a. Complicité
   b. Frantic Assembly
   c. Royal Shakespeare Company
   d. National Youth Theatre

Short Answer Questions

4. How does the play reflect early 2000s discussions about autism and inclusion in schools?
5. Why does Siobhan, rather than Christopher himself, to deliver parts of the narration to the audience?
6. How does the Boone family's story reflect wider social changes in Britain in the early 2000s?

The Curious Incident of the Dog in the Night-time

Context-Based Tasks

7. Explain how the staging of *The Curious Incident of the Dog in the Night-time* helps the audience to experience Christopher's unique perspective. In your answer, refer to at least two techniques (e.g. ensemble movement, projections, sound effects, or the grid-like stage design).
8. Write a short paragraph explaining how an audience in the early 2000s might respond to Christopher's determination to travel alone to London.

Chapter 5
Main Themes and Key Quotes

The Curious Incident of the Dog in the Night-time explores how Christopher makes sense of a world that often feels overwhelming. Through his perspective, ordinary moments become problems to solve or patterns to trust, so themes like honesty, communication, family, courage, and discovery feel immediate and concrete.

This guide presents seven key themes. For each one, you'll see how the idea develops across the play, how staging and structure shape the audience's response, and how to turn that insight into exam-ready analysis. These themes are connected where a single moment can relate to trust, family, and independence all together. Strong essays will show that you understand these connections and are able to use precise evidence to build a focused argument.

In Section A of the Edexcel IGCSE English Literature Paper 2, you are expected to engage closely with the text and support your points using specific evidence. At the end of each theme is a selection of key quotations from *The Curious Incident of the Dog in the Night-time*, relevant to the theme, with brief annotations and guidance on how to remember and use them effectively in exam responses.

While you are allowed to take a clean copy of the play into the exam, familiarity with key lines improves speed, confidence, and the ability to write fluent, structured responses.

Honesty and Trust

[Includes truth, lies, communication, reliability, misunderstanding]

Overview

Honesty and trust underpin every relationship in the play. Secrets cause confusion and pain, while truth and openness rebuild connection.

How It Is Developed

- For Christopher, honesty is absolute; lies disrupt the order that keeps him safe.
- He finds metaphors difficult to understand because they make no literal sense. In his perception, metaphors distort or hide meaning.
- Ed's lies about Judy and Wellington challenge Christopher's trust and sense of safety.
- Christopher's physical reaction (vomiting) emphasises his shock at the betrayal.
- Judy avoids confronting her guilt and sense of inadequacy as a mother, believing Ed understands Christopher better.

- Siobhan communicates calmly and clearly, becoming a model of reliability.
- His book, read aloud by Siobhan, becomes his most assured way of telling the truth.

Evolution Through the Plot

As the play develops, honesty moves from a personal need to a test of care and understanding. The adults in Christopher's world hide the truth to 'protect' him. They eventually learn that honesty is essential to trust. In writing down his story, he defines truth through his own evidence and observation.

Key Quotes

"It is because I can't tell lies." — Christopher
Christopher defines honesty as a personal rule, setting up truth as the foundation of his identity and the play's central conflict.

"I think it should be called a lie because a pig is not like a day and people do not have skeletons in their cupboards." — Christopher
His literal approach to language turns metaphors into falsehoods, making ordinary communication uncertain.

"I do not tell lies. Mother used to say that this was because I was a good person." — Christopher
Links truthfulness to moral goodness and parental approval. The line introduces emotional complexity to Christopher's honesty.

The Curious Incident of the Dog in the Night-time

"I find people confusing." — Christopher
Christopher's difficulty in interpreting tone and emotion exposes how human communication often hides meaning rather than clarifying it.

"I see everything." — Christopher
A recurring motif of precision and observation; his factual clarity contrasts with adults' selective honesty.

"Father said you were dead. But he lied." — Christopher
The blunt factual delivery of this line heightens the emotional force of betrayal and the breakdown of trust within his family.

"I did it for your own good, Christopher. Honestly, I did." — Ed
The ironic "honestly" underscores how adults justify deceit as protection, revealing moral inconsistency.

"Did it make you sad to find out your mother and Mr. Shears had an affair?" — Siobhan
Siobhan's clarity and empathy create a safe space for truth and emotional understanding.

"It's bloody hard telling the truth all the time." — Ed
Ed acknowledges that the truth is important to Christopher even though it is difficult for him to practise.

"You have to learn to trust me... and I don't care how long it takes." — Ed
Ed's persistence and sincerity show that trust, once broken, can only return through patience and honesty.

Tip to Remember: Use these quotations when writing about honesty, truth, and lies, metaphors, and the contrast between communication breakdown and moments of clarity.

✏️ Quick Recap: Why are metaphors confusing to Christopher?

✏️ Extension Task: Write a short paragraph explaining how honesty affects Christopher's relationships with Ed, Judy, and Siobhan. Use one quotation to support your answer.

Family, Love, and Care

[Includes parenting, attachment, relationships, dependence, loyalty, separation, reconciliation]

Overview

Love and care are central to the family's relationships even though they are not always demonstrated in healthy or conventional ways.

How It Is Developed

- Ed's version of love means providing structure and protection through daily routines.
- His lies about Judy and Wellington damages Christopher's trust and sense of safety.
- Judy admits her failings as a mother but her love is never doubted, as she seeks to rebuild her relationship through honesty and patience.
- Christopher's logical thinking limits how he recognises emotion, yet he values dependable actions.

- Siobhan provides calm, consistent care and reassurance that other adults are unable to provide.
- Toby represents loyalty and comfort symbolising unconditional attachment.

Evolution Through the Plot

Ed's practical care first defines love and safety for Christopher, but his deceit exposes its fragility. Judy's love as a mother is unwavering although her actions reveal her frustrations. For the family, love is imperfect but enduring.

Key Quotes

"You're not to go asking Mrs Shears who killed that bloody dog." — Ed
Ed tries to protect Christopher by controlling what he does and hears, showing his mix of care and frustration.

"I love you very much, Christopher. Don't ever forget that." — Ed
Simple, direct language conveys deep affection and a wish for reassurance.

"You have to know that I am going to tell you the truth from now on." — Ed
Promises consistency and marks the first step toward rebuilding trust.

"I was not a very good mother, Christopher. Maybe if things had been different, maybe if you'd been different." — Judy
Expresses regret and longing to reconnect; repetition of 'maybe' conveys uncertainty.

"I'm sorry, Christopher. I never meant to hurt you." — Judy
The plainness of the language communicates honesty and affection, restoring emotional contact between mother and son.

"I like it when you read to me. And I like it when you play with me." — Christopher
Describes love through shared time and care rather than verbal declarations.

"I'm going to live with Mother." — Christopher
Demonstrates agency and self-determination. This statement reflects his logical reasoning and emotional growth as he decides what kind of family structure feels safe and right for him.

"You'll catch your death out here." — Judy
An instinctive phrase of maternal concern that re-establishes her role as a caring parent and hints at the ease with which family intimacy can return.

"I could make them let me take Toby." — Christopher
Toby represents unconditional loyalty and comfort. His presence provides emotional security when human relationships feel uncertain.

Tip to Remember: Use these quotations when exploring family bonds, love, care, separation, reconciliation, and how honesty helps family members understand one another.

✏ Quick Recap: How do Ed and Judy each try to protect Christopher, and how do their choices affect his trust?

The Curious Incident of the Dog in the Night-time

🖊 **Extension Task:** Write a diary entry from Christopher after reading Judy's letters. How does he express his feelings about his parents? Use at least one quote to support your answer.

Courage and Independence

[Includes bravery, persistence, resilience, self-belief, growth]

Overview

Courage and independence do not come naturally to Christopher. It is only when he has no other choice that he finds the courage to pursue his desires independently.

How It Is Developed

- Christopher's desire to solve Wellington's murder forces him to interact with neighbours and strangers even though he finds people confusing.
- Travelling to London becomes a major test of courage and independence.
- He uses logic to manage fear in unfamiliar places and situations.
- Excelling at his maths exam shows that he can set goals and succeed on his own.

Evolution Through the Plot

Courage and independence progresses from small steps into major decisions. At first, Christopher takes measured risks, asking questions, breaking rules, and recording what he sees. The journey to London forces him into unfamiliar places, where he uses logic and memory to manage fear. Siobhan's voice keeps him steady when the world feels out of control. In completing his exam and making his own choices, Christopher learns that courage and independence mean trusting that he knows he can achieve whatever he puts his mind to.

Key Quotes

"I'm going to find out who killed Wellington." — Christopher
His decision to investigate Wellington's death defines his character and introduces courage as action

"I find people confusing." — Christopher
His honesty about confusion highlights the strength it takes to engage with the world on his own terms.

"I don't talk to strangers." — Christopher
His decision to continue questioning neighbours despite this fear reveals how courage grows through persistence.

"Does that mean I can do anything?" — Christopher
Courage becomes part of his identity, transforming fear into confidence and independence.

Tip to Remember

Use these quotations when writing about bravery, persistence, and how Christopher learns to rely on himself.

✏ Quick Recap: What does Christopher describe as his first act of bravery?

✏ Extension Task: Write a diary entry in which Christopher explains why bravery is important for achieving independence. Include at least one quotation.

Loss and Grief

[Includes absence, betrayal, regret, change, recovery]

Overview

Loss and grief in the play demonstrate how both affects people, how they respond, and how their relationships are shaped. It also highlights how differently Christopher reacts, often through logic and action rather than emotion.

How It Is Developed

- Wellington's death introduces the theme of loss and begins Christopher's investigation.
- Ed's sense of loss when Judy leaves drives his anger and dishonesty.
- Judy describes her sense of loss, both in leaving Christopher and in her failure to cope as a mother.
- Christopher's greatest loss is when he learns that Ed has lied and realises he can no longer trust him.
- Grief underlines the moments of regret and apology, as characters attempt to repair broken bonds.

Evolution Through the Plot

The play opens with Wellington's death, which is shocking to the audience (and community) and sets the mystery in motion. This loss is paralleled by Judy's absence, which Christopher accepts in a very detached manner until he reads her letters.

Ed's grief at Judy's departure drives his lies and destructive choices. For Christopher, the greatest loss is from Ed's dishonesty about Judy's leaving and Wellington's death.

Key Quotes

"The dog is dead." — Christopher
His detached tone contrasts with the emotions that the audience would attach to death.

"Father said you were dead. But he lied." — Christopher
His flat delivery heightens the sense of betrayal and absence.

"I went to London because I couldn't cope any more, because I felt lonely and I was with Mr Shears." — Judy (letter)
Judy's feelings of isolation and desire to be noticed contributed to the family breakdown.

"I was not a very good mother, Christopher. Maybe if things had been different, maybe if you'd been different." — Judy
The repetition of "maybe" captures Judy's grief at the state of their relationship.

"I'm sorry, Christopher. I never meant to hurt you." — Judy
Judy's apology highlights how much loss and grief has affected her emotionally.

"I need to take Toby with me." — Christopher
Toby symbolises stability and comfort to Christopher and he cannot bear to part with him.

Tip to Remember

Use these quotes when writing about death, absence, or betrayal.

🖉 Quick Recap: How does Wellington's death set the theme of loss in motion?

🖉 Reflection Prompt: Why might Christopher describe loss in such a factual way?

🖉 Extension Task: Write a short piece from Judy's perspective, explaining how she feels about the time she lost with Christopher. Include at least one quotation.

Anger and Conflict

[Includes frustration, guilt, misunderstanding, tension, resolution]

Overview

Anger and conflict influence how the characters communicate, respond to pressure, and navigate relationships. Tension builds as truths are hidden or revealed, and moments of confrontation reveal deeper feelings of guilt, fear, or loss. As Christopher finds raised voices and sudden emotion overwhelming, conflict causes confusion and danger in his world.

How It Is Developed

- Ed loses his temper when Christopher ignores him and continues to investigate Wellington's death.
- The conflict between Ed and Judy is highlighted in their separation and their arguments about parenting.
- Christopher reacts to conflict by withdrawing
- Staging intensifies conflict through movement, sound,

and physical interaction, creating disruption and tension.

Evolution Through the Plot

Conflict begins early when Ed shouts at Christopher for asking too many questions. It intensifies when Ed strikes him, demonstrating the destructive impact of frustration. Judy's letters reveal the conflict she felt within the family and explain her decision to leave. Although Ed reveals his lies about Judy and Wellington calmly, the conflict is so significant that Christopher needs to leave home.

Key Quotes

"Just try and keep your nose out of other people's business."
— Ed
Ed's frustration is clear in his sharp tone and it foreshadows the pattern of conflict that will grow between father and son.

"You're not listening, are you, Christopher?" — Ed
Ed mistakes Christopher's silence for disobedience, while the audience recognises Christopher's need for time to process, heightening dramatic irony.

"Don't give me that bollocks. You knew exactly what you were bloody doing." — Ed
Ed's use of expletives reflects his anger and frustration. uncontrolled anger and loss of restraint

"I'm sorry I hit you. I didn't mean to. I love you very much." — Ed
The pacing conveys genuine remorse and emotional exhaustion,

"...when the red mist comes down..." — Ed
The metaphor captures Ed's loss of control when he is angry.

Tip to Remember

Use these quotations to analyse how anger is a force that influences choices, damages trust, and exposes underlying truths.

🖊 Quick Recap: How does Ed's anger affect Christopher?

🖊 Extension Task: Write a short scene imagining an argument between Judy and Ed before she left. Focus on words or actions that show frustration and tension.

Order and Chaos

[Includes logic, confusion, control, structure, perception]

Overview

Although order and chaos are direct opposites, both are central to how Christopher views the world. Order through routines, logic, and patterns, helps him feel secure while chaos in the form of dishonesty, unexpected events, and disruptive environments confuse and overwhelm him.

How It Is Developed

- Christopher finds comfort in order through maths, prime numbers, maps, and routines.
- His investigation into Wellington's death introduces chaos, drawing him into arguments and difficult truths.
- The train station and London are staged as overwhelming spaces filled with noise, movement, and disorder.
- Family breakdown represents emotional chaos, disrupting Christopher's sense of stability.
- Christopher finds new ways to impose order, such as writing his book, caring for Toby, and completing his A-level.

Evolution Through the Plot

At the start, everything is ordered in Christopher's world. However as he investigates and uncovers more difficult truths, what he once believed to be true and safe is no longer. His need to find Judy despite the challenging journey introduces more chaos than he has ever experienced. His persistence and determination help him focus on what he can control and learn to ignore the chaos around him.

Key Quotes

"My name is Christopher John Francis Boone. I know all the countries of the world and the capital cities. And every prime number up to 7,507." — Christopher
Christopher relies on facts and ordered knowledge to make sense of his world.

The Curious Incident of the Dog in the Night-time

"The dog is dead." — Christopher
This blunt observation signals the disruption of his ordered world. The simple factual statement marks the entry of chaos into the story.

"I see everything." — Christopher
Suggests both clarity and overload: his detailed perception can restore order or become overwhelming.

"Does that mean I can do anything?" — Christopher
Suggests that order has been restored through his own achievements. The question reflects hope and possibility after chaos and uncertainty.

Tip to Remember

Use these ideas to explain how structure and confusion are presented in both the play's staging and in Christopher's development.

✏ *Reflection Prompt:* In what ways does Christopher strive for order in a world that he cannot fully control?

✏ *Extension Task:* Write a short analysis describing how lighting, sound, or projection in the play symbolises the tension between order and chaos.

Adventure and Discovery

[Includes curiosity, investigation, learning, self-realisation, achievement]

Overview

Adventure and discovery drive the play's action and emotional development. Christopher's adventure becomes a test of courage and independence, while discovery transforms how he sees himself and those around him. Each new experience, planned or accidental, forces him to navigate an unpredictable world, building his understanding of trust, resilience, and possibility.

How It Is Developed

- The investigation into Wellington's death begins as a detective story, giving Christopher a sense of purpose and control.
- Christopher's search for his notebook leads to Judy's letters and Ed's confession, reshaping his beliefs and family.
- Travelling to London is a major adventure, staged through movement, sound, and confusion to reflect his sensory challenge.
- Speaking to strangers, navigating train stations, and rescuing Toby all test his ability to adapt and persevere.
- His A-level achievement proves to himself that he can meet new challenges and succeed.

Evolution Through the Plot

Christopher's adventure begins with curiosity and logic as Wellington's death becomes a puzzle to solve. As his journey unfolds, logic alone no longer protects him and his discoveries become emotional as he faces betrayal, fear, and uncertainty. His physical journey from Swindon to London mirrors his growth from dependence to self-direction.

Key Quotes (in order of appearance, with notes)

"I'm going to find out who killed Wellington." — Christopher
Highlights his resolve and determination.

"This is a murder mystery novel." — Christopher
Christopher's book allows him control over his own story and narrative

"I decided that I was going to do some detecting." — Christopher
He frames his journey as a detective story, turning real life into an adventure he can manage.

"I found the letters in the shirt box in Father's room." — Christopher
The simple narrative belies the emotional trauma when he realises Ed has been lying.

"Does that mean I can do anything?" — Christopher
The question suggests that his adventure has expanded his sense of what is now achievable.

Tip to Remember

Use these quotations to analyse how how Christopher navigates unfamiliar surroundings, including physical journeys and new experiences.

✏ Quick Recap: What event begins Christopher's adventure?

✏ Discuss: Is Christopher's greatest discovery about his family, or about himself? Give reasons for your answer.

Themes	Christopher	Ed	Judy	Siobhan	Mrs Alexander	Mrs Shears	Mr Shears
Honesty and Trust	✓	✓	✓	✓	✓	✓	✓
Family, Love and Care	✓	✓	✓	✓	✓	✓	✓
Courage and Independence	✓	✓	✓	✓			
Loss and Grief	✓	✓	✓			✓	
Anger and Conflict	✓	✓	✓				
Order and Chaos	✓	✓	✓	✓			
Adventure and Discovery	✓	✓	✓	✓	✓		

Table 1. This character-theme matrix summarises which themes are most closely associated with each key figure in *The Curious Incident of the Dog in the Night-time*.

How to Write About Themes in The Curious Incident of the Dog in the Night-time

Most exam questions will ask you to explore either a character or a theme. Even if the question focuses on a character, strong answers often include reference to key themes — such as honesty, betrayal, family, or independence.

To succeed, your writing should:

- Show an understanding of how the theme is developed across the play (AO1)
- Explain how language, structure, staging, or character interaction is used to present that theme (AO2)
- Offer an interpretation — not just what happens, but why it matters and how the audience is expected to respond.

Simple Writing Frame

The theme of [theme] is explored through [character/action/scene] by [technique, e.g. structure, staging, language].

This highlights [effect on the audience or significance in the play], especially when [quotation/example].

Sample Paragraph – Theme of Courage and Independence

The theme of *courage and independence* is explored in Christopher's decision to leave home and travel to London alone. The moment he leaves his home for the train station marks a turning point, he acts without guidance or comfort, relying on logic and observation to manage fear. Through fast movement, lighting changes, and overlapping voices, the staging captures his confusion and the scale of what he must face. His persistence in completing the journey demonstrates (This highlights) his courage as determination rather than confidence. By the end of the play, his question, *"Does that mean I can do anything?"* reflects the independence he has earned and his belief in new possibilities.

📌 **Exam Tips:**

- Avoid just listing themes. Focus on how one idea is developed through a specific moment, character, or staging choice.
- Link every quote back to Christopher's perspective and/or the audience's response.
- Use confident verbs: *presents, develops, highlights, reveals, emphasises, suggests.*
- Remember that form and staging choices (e.g. narration, ensemble, projections, sound) are as important as language when writing about this play.

The Curious Incident of the Dog in the Night-time

Self-Test Block: Main Themes

Use this self-test block to consolidate your understanding of the main themes in *The Curious Incident of the Dog in the Night-time*. This includes a mix of multiple-choice questions, short answer prompts, and theme-based tasks.

Multiple Choice Questions

1. Which theme is introduced by Christopher's blunt statement, *"The dog is dead"*?
   a. Adventure and Discovery
   b. Loss and Grief
   c. Anger and Conflict
   d. Order and Chaos
2. Which character most clearly represents stability and calm communication for Christopher?
   a. Ed
   b. Judy
   c. Siobhan
   d. Mrs Shears
3. The theme of trust is most severely tested when:
   a. Judy admits her guilt in a letter
   b. Ed reveals the truth about Wellington
   c. Siobhan reads from Christopher's book
   d. Mrs Alexander speaks to Christopher in the street
4. Which theme is emphasised through the chaotic staging of the London Underground scene?
   a. Courage and independence
   b. Family and Relationships
   c. Love and Attachment
   d. Loss and Grief

5. Which quotation best expresses the theme of discovery?
   a. "I decided that I was going to do some detecting."
   b. "I need to take Toby with me."
   c. "Father said you were dead. But he lied."
   d. "I was not a very good mother, Christopher."
6. Which theme is most clearly reflected in Christopher's use of prime numbers and logical patterns?
   a. Adventure and Discovery
   b. Order and Chaos
   c. Anger and Conflict
   d. Loss and Grief

Short Answer Questions

7. How does Siobhan help Christopher navigate communication?
8. How does the London train station scene highlight Christopher's struggle between order and chaos?
9. Select a quote that represents Judy's attempt at reconciliation. What theme does it link to, and how does it affect the audience?

The Curious Incident of the Dog in the Night-time

Longer Tasks

10. Write a paragraph explaining how the theme of honesty and trust change from the beginning to the end of the play. Refer to one quotation in your answer.

11. Choose two of the following themes:
    - Family and Relationships
    - Courage and Independence
    - Love, Care, and Attachment
    - Anger and Conflict

For each one, write a short paragraph (3-5 sentences) explaining:

- How one character reflects this theme
- One quote that supports your idea
- Why the theme is presented in this way

Chapter 6
Glossary of Key Literary and Dramatic Terms

In order to write clearly, critically, and convincingly about *The Curious Incident of the Dog in the Night-time*, you need to use the language of literary analysis. Examiners expect you to identify and comment on how the play uses form, structure, staging, and language to shape meaning. This glossary provides definitions of the most relevant terms for analysing dramatic texts at GCSE and IGCSE level.

These terms will help you analyse techniques precisely and meet the requirements of AO2: analysing language, form, and structure. Use this glossary to revise key concepts and improve the depth of your responses. You do not need to memorise every definition. Focus on the ones that best help you explain *how* the play creates meaning and *why* the audience responds as it does.

Language Techniques

Emotive language
Words chosen to provoke an emotional response.

Euphemism
A mild or indirect expression used in place of something harsh or blunt.

Hyperbole
Exaggeration for emphasis or dramatic effect.

Juxtaposition
Placing contrasting ideas or moods side by side.

Literalism
Speaking or interpreting language in a strictly factual way.

Metaphor
A direct comparison between two unrelated things.

Monologue
A long speech by one character expressing thoughts or feelings.

Narration
Direct address or commentary guiding the audience through events.

Repetition
The repeated use of a word or phrase for emphasis or rhythm.

Simile
A comparison using "like" or "as."

Symbolism
Using an object, image, or action to represent a larger idea.

Tone
The attitude or emotional quality conveyed by the writer or a character.

Structure and Plot

Cyclical structure
The play returns to earlier moments or ideas, creating a sense of completion.

Contrast between calm and chaos
Alternating stillness and movement to reflect tension or emotion.

Delayed revelation
Withholding information to build suspense or shape audience understanding.

Ensemble movement
Actors working together to create setting, atmosphere, or physical storytelling.

Flashback
A scene or memory from the past presented within the main timeline.

The Curious Incident of the Dog in the Night-time

Foreshadowing
Hints or clues about events that will occur later in the play.

Framing device
A story-within-a-story structure that shapes how events are told.

Motif
A recurring image, symbol, or idea that reinforces a central theme.

Non-linear structure
Events arranged out of chronological order.

Sequential revelations
Plot developments are revealed step-by-step to build suspense.

Pacing
The speed and rhythm at which scenes unfold; faster pacing increases tension or chaos.

Parallel action
Simultaneous or overlapping action and narration.

Real-time narrative
Action that unfolds at the same pace as 'real life'.

Withholding information
Delaying key truths to build tension or control audience awareness.

Dramatic Form and Devices

Choral speech
Ensemble voices speaking together to create atmosphere or intensity.

Direct address
A character speaks directly to the audience, breaking the boundary of performance. (see also Fourth wall).

Exposition
Background information revealed through narration or dialogue.

Fourth wall
The imaginary wall between the audience and the actors; breaking it engages the audience directly.

Projection
Use of light, images, or text to visualise thoughts or setting.

Physical theatre
Expressive movement used to tell the story physically.

Soundscape
Layered sound or voices creating mood and sensory experience.

Stage directions
Instructions in the script about movement, expression, lighting, or setting.

Subtext
The underlying meaning behind a character's words or actions.

Theatrical devices
Techniques used to enhance the audience's experience (e.g., lighting, pauses, props).

Literary Concepts and Critical Terms

Allusion
A brief reference to another text, event, or cultural idea.

Conflict
The tension or struggle between characters or opposing forces.

Identity
How a character understands or defines who they are.

Perspective
The viewpoint from which a story or scene is presented.

Protagonist
The main character who drives the action.

Reliability
How far a narrator's account can be trusted or accepted as accurate.

Resilience
The capacity to recover or persist in the face of difficulty.

Social context
The social, cultural, or historical background influencing a text.

Theme
A central idea or message explored in the play.

Using This Glossary as You Write

This glossary gives you the vocabulary to write clearly and accurately about *The Curious Incident of the Dog in the Night-time*. Each term helps you explain how language, dramatic form, structure, and staging are used to create meaning in the play.

You are **not expected to memorise or use every single term**. Start by focusing on the terms that help you explain the play's techniques precisely. For *Curious Incident*, pay special attention to words like narration, framing device, ensemble movement, projection, and motif, as these are particularly valuable.

Use this glossary whenever you plan or review your work. You'll find it especially helpful in the sections that follow, on structure, analysis, and essay writing. Over time, using these terms will make your writing more confident and analytical, showing examiners that you understand the story and the way it is presented.

Self-test: Glossary of Literary and Dramatic Terms

Multiple Choice Questions

Choose the most accurate answer for each question:

1. Christopher's line *"The dog is dead"* is an example of:
    a. Emotive language
    b. Literalism
    c. Hyperbole
    d. Symbolism
2. Which term best describes Christopher's book, read aloud by Siobhan throughout the play?
    a. Flashback
    b. Framing device
    c. Monologue
    d. Real-time narrative
3. Which of these is a **motif** in the play?
    a. Christopher's narration
    b. The dining table
    c. Prime numbers
    d. A wedding ring

Short Answer Questions

Answer each in one or two sentences:

4. What is the difference between *narration* and *dialogue* in the play?
5. Give one example of *symbolism* in *Curious Incident* and explain what it represents.
6. Why is *ensemble movement* important in showing Christopher's perspective?

Fill in the Blanks

7. A _____ is a repeated image or phrase that helps reinforce a theme.
8. The term _____ _____ refers to a moment when Christopher or Siobhan speak directly to the audience.
9. Projection is used to show Christopher's _____ on stage.

Reflection Prompt

10. Which three terms from the glossary do you find most useful for analysing *Curious Incident*, and how will you apply them in your next essay?

Chapter 7
Language, Form and Structure

Section A of the Edexcel IGCSE English Literature Paper 2 explicitly requires you to analyse how writers use language, form, and structure to create meanings and effects. This is the essence of Assessment Objective 2 (AO2) and is present in every exam question, regardless of theme or character focus.

This section explores how specific techniques are used in *The Curious Incident of the Dog in the Night-time* to shape the play's impact, reflect Christopher's unique perspective, and influence the audience.

When writing about *The Curious Incident of the Dog in the Night-time*, remember it is a play written for performance. You are analysing the dialogue, language and stagecraft. Also pay attention to details such as how lighting, projection, soundscapes, and ensemble movement shape audience response.

How to Use This Section

This chapter includes a wide range of techniques, more than you will ever need in any one essay. You are not expected to use every idea. Start with a few techniques that you understand clearly and practise writing about them. In your exam, focus on just a small number of your favourite techniques and connect them directly to the question and theme.

Language

The language choices in the play reflect both Christopher's literal, factual perspective and the emotional struggles of the adults around him. Simple, blunt statements often carry great weight, while other moments use repetition, fragmented sentences, and symbolism to reveal deeper feelings.

The list below provides the name of a language technique compared to its example and the effect it causes. This list is very comprehensive and by no means all necessary at IGCSE level. We would recommend picking out a few of your favourites and committing them to memory. With time and practise, you will start to find it easier to recognise and name these when you are reading the text.

Key Techniques and Examples

Apology and regret
"I was not a very good mother." — Judy
Effect: Expresses accountability and emotional honesty; reveals Judy's attempt to make peace and restore connection.

Colloquial speech
"Just try and keep your nose out of other people's business." — Ed
Effect: Reflects working-class realism and impatience; conveys authority and emotional volatility.

Contrast in tone
Siobhan's calm narration vs Ed's aggression
Effect: Emphasises emotional imbalance; deepens audience empathy and awareness of Christopher's sensory world.

Dialogue
Naturalistic exchanges between characters.
Effect: Builds authenticity and tension; exposes relationships and communication breakdowns.

Emotive language
"I never meant to hurt you." — Judy
Effect: Creates pathos and emotional intimacy; invites the audience to understand her guilt and vulnerability.

Euphemism
"I couldn't cope." — Judy
Effect: Softens painful truth; reveals avoidance and emotional repression.

Explicit language
"Don't give me that bollocks." / "What the hell were you doing?" — Ed
Effect: Heightens realism and tension; conveys anger and loss of control.

Figurative language
Judy's letters use figurative expressions of emotion.
Effect: Conveys loneliness and frustration; contrasts with Christopher's logical voice.

Fragmented sentences
"Just...let me explain. When your mum left..." — Ed
Effect: Suggests panic and guilt; reflects emotional strain and hesitation.

Irony
"Honestly I did." — Ed
Effect: Undermines credibility; exposes self-justification and moral tension.

Literalism
"The dog is dead." — Christopher
Effect: Establishes his factual mindset; heightens contrast between logic and emotion.

Metaphor
Judy's letters use metaphors about loneliness and failure.
Effect: Expresses emotional depth and regret; highlights contrast with Christopher's literal world.

Repetition
"I want to go to London." "I want to go to London." — Christopher
Effect: Reinforces determination and control; mirrors his focus and persistence.

The Curious Incident of the Dog in the Night-time

Rhetorical question
"Does that mean I can do anything?" — Christopher
Effect: Marks personal growth and curiosity; invites reflection on independence and possibility.

Sarcasm
"Well it's nice to know my contribution is appreciated." – Mr Shears
Effect: Reveals defensiveness and resentment; exposes tension and emotional distance.

Short sentences
"The dog is dead." / "I don't like strangers."
Effect: Creates immediacy and tension; reflects Christopher's clarity and directness.

Symbolism
Toby the rat
Effect: Symbolises safety and continuity; represents emotional comfort in an unstable world.

Tone and register shifts
Siobhan's calm reassurance vs Ed's angry shouting.
Effect: Highlights emotional contrast; illustrates the balance between support and conflict in Christopher's relationships.

Understatement
"I was quite upset." — Christopher
Effect: Minimises emotion to maintain control; accentuates his difficulty expressing feelings.

📌 **Exam Tip:** Focus on how language choices within the play create tone and character. For top marks, always explain *why* a word or phrase is effective, not just what it means.

Sentence Starters for Writing About Language

These sentence frames can help you write about how language is used effectively in the play.

The [technique] used in the play reinforces/shows/highlights... [effect]

- The word/phrase "[quote]" suggests...
- This creates a feeling of...
- This helps the audience understand...
- This reflects the theme of...
- The tone of this line conveys...
- The contrast between [X] and [Y] emphasises...

This supports the theme of...

Tip: Use one or two of these language techniques when writing about a character or theme. Keep your sentences clear and precise, and avoid listing techniques without explaining their impact.

How to Apply a Language Technique in an Essay

Knowing the language technique is only part of AO2, you also need to be able to explain how it works in the play and what effect it has. Here's an example of how to write about language using a clear, exam-style paragraph.

Literalism and rhetorical questions are used effectively in the play to characterise Christopher's growth. At the beginning of the play, when Christopher bluntly observes, *"The dog is dead,"* the factual tone reflects his way of processing the world. By the end, his question, *"Does that mean I can do anything?"* marks growing independence and belief in possibility. These contrasting moments use language to show Christopher's development and invite the audience to admire his determination.

🖊 Extension Challenge

1. Choose a quote by Ed or Judy. Identify the technique (e.g. repetition, emotive language), then write a short paragraph explaining how it affects the audience and connects to a theme.
2. How might the play feel different if Christopher used more figurative language? Rewrite one of his blunt statements as a metaphor and comment on how this changes its meaning and tone.

Form

The Curious Incident of the Dog in the Night-time is presented as a **play-within-a-play**, adapted by Simon Stephens and developed in collaboration with **Frantic Assembly**. The production combines narration, projection, and physical theatre to stage Christopher's inner world and to show how he experiences reality.

Understanding the **form** of the play means looking beyond dialogue to consider how theatrical techniques such as movement, lighting, sound, and staging to communicate meaning. These elements shape the audience's understanding of Christopher's thoughts and emotions as much as the words themselves. You do not need to remember every device, but focus on a few that you can confidently link to a theme, moment, or audience response.

Dramatic Form Features

Choral speech
Ensemble voices speak or echo together to create atmosphere, energy, or confusion.

Direct address
Christopher and Siobhan speak directly to the audience, breaking the fourth wall and drawing them into his world.

Entrances and exits
Characters appear or reappear at key moments, marking emotional turning points or shifts in tension.

Framing device / play-within-a-play
Christopher's book is read aloud by Siobhan and staged as part of the performance, keeping the story within his perspective.

Lighting shifts
Changes in brightness and colour signal mood, focus, or emotional transition.

The Curious Incident of the Dog in the Night-time

Minimal props
Simple cubes and objects transform into furniture, barriers, or locations, supporting a non-naturalistic, imaginative style.

Non-naturalistic form
Combines realistic dialogue with stylised movement, sound, and design to explore Christopher's inner world.

Real-time sequences
Certain scenes, such as the train journey, unfold moment by moment to build tension and realism.

Open ending
Christopher's closing question, "Does that mean I can do anything?", leaves the audience reflecting on his growth and uncertainty.

Projection and multimedia
Images, words, and maps are projected on stage to represent Christopher's thoughts, logic, and perception of space.

Physical theatre / Ensemble movement
Actors use coordinated movement and lifts to form settings or express emotion, influenced by Frantic Assembly's style.

Silence and pause
Moments of stillness follow shock or discovery, allowing emotion and tension to register.

Soundscape
Layered voices and sound effects recreate sensory overload and immerse the audience in Christopher's experience.

Stage directions

Detailed notes on movement, projection, and sound guide performance and emphasise theatrical storytelling.

Sentence Starters for Writing About Form

These sentence starters will help you write clearly about how the **form and staging** of the play create meaning and shape the audience's response. They are useful for explaining how movement, lighting, sound, or projection contribute to the play's impact and connect to themes.

The use of [device] in this scene emphasises / highlights / creates...

- *This technique helps the audience to experience...*
- *The [form] of/in the play allows the audience to see / understand...*
- *The choice of [staging / movement / projection] reflects...*
- *The moment when [describe action] has the effect of...*

The physical or visual elements in this scene convey...

Tip: When writing about a character or theme, aim to include one or two references to how the play's form supports the ideas you are analysing.

How to Apply a Form Feature in an Essay

Being able to identify the form features in the play is important but you will also need to be able to explain **how** the form is used in the play and **what effect** it has on the audience. The example below models a clear, exam-style paragraph.

The use of ensemble movement and sound in the train station scene captures Christopher's experience of chaos. The ensemble crowd around him with overlapping voices and sharp physical movements, creating a soundscape of panic and confusion. This moment immerses the audience in Christopher's perspective and highlights his determination to remain calm despite deep fear. The staging turns an ordinary journey into a test of courage, showing how theatrical form communicates emotion and tension beyond dialogue.

📌 **Exam Tip:**

Focus on how a particular theatrical form influences the audience. For example, how does ensemble movement reveal his sense of isolation or confusion?

✏️ **Discuss:**

Discuss with a partner: Why might the production use physical theatre and projections instead of realistic sets? How does this choice help the audience understand Christopher's perspective?

Structure

The structure of *The Curious Incident of the Dog in the Night-time* reflects Christopher's way of thinking, logical, step by step, yet interrupted by revelation and disorder. The play moves between routine and disruption, mirroring how Christopher processes the world around him. Large-scale structural choices, such as the non-linear framing and delayed revelations, combined with smaller patterns of repetition and motif to guide the audience's understanding.

Recognising how these techniques work will strengthen your AO2 analysis and help you write about the play with precision.

This list includes the most important structural elements to know. You do not need to memorise them all. Focus on a few that are clear to you and practise using them confidently in your writing.

Structural features

Cliffhanger moment
Example: Christopher fleeing after finding the letters.
Purpose/Effect: Builds suspense and shifts focus from solving the mystery to confronting family truth.

Contrast and juxtaposition
Example: Quiet mathematical reflection against the chaos of the train station.
Purpose/Effect: Highlights Christopher's struggle between order and sensory confusion.

Cyclical ending
Example: Christopher closes the play with his book and exam result.
Purpose/Effect: Restores order and confidence; suggests resolution through learning and independence.

Delayed revelation
Example: The truth about Judy and Mr Shears is revealed gradually.
Purpose/Effect: Increases dramatic tension and draws the audience into Christopher's emotional discovery.

Exposition through narration
Example: Christopher introduces himself and the mystery directly to the audience.
Purpose/Effect: Provides clarity and immediacy; establishes his narrative control.

Foreshadowing
Example: Ed's defensive tone about Mrs Shears.
Purpose/Effect: Creates dramatic irony and prepares the audience for later confession.

Motif
Example: Prime numbers, maps, and mathematical patterns.
Purpose/Effect: Reinforces order and logic; symbolises stability in a chaotic world.

Non-linear narrative
Example: Flashbacks and letters interrupt chronological order.
Purpose/Effect: Reflects the layered process of discovery and the workings of memory.

Parallel action
Example: Narration overlaps with staged movement and projection.
Purpose/Effect: Merges storytelling and performance, immersing the audience in Christopher's perspective.

Real-time action
Example: The train station sequence unfolding second by second.
Purpose/Effect: Builds intensity and urgency; allows the audience to share Christopher's sensory experience.

Repetition and echoing
Example: Phrases such as "I can do anything" recur throughout.
Purpose/Effect: Emphasises growth and determination; reinforces themes of progress and resilience.

Sequential revelations
Example: Mystery solved step by step — Wellington → Judy's letters → Ed's confession.
Purpose/Effect: Sustains narrative momentum and mirrors the logical structure of detective fiction.

Sentence Starters for Writing About Structure

These sentence starters can help you write about how the **structure** of the play shapes meaning and influences the audience's understanding. They are useful for linking **sequence, pattern, or contrast** to key ideas, moments, or emotions in the play.

Useful starters include:

The structure of the play highlights / reflects / builds...

- *The use of [technique] in this moment creates the effect of...*
- *The play's organisation around [motif / revelation / contrast] emphasises...*
- *The word or phrase "[quote]" suggests...*
- *This sequence helps the audience to understand...*
- *The placement of this scene / event reinforces...*
- *The repetition or return to [idea / phrase] underlines...*

The structure encourages the audience to notice / anticipate / question...

When writing about structure, aim to explain **how and why** events are arranged in this way and what effect this has on the audience.

📌 **Exam Tip:**

When analysing structure, focus on how the play **builds or releases tension**, **reveals information**, or **returns to earlier ideas**. Look for patterns such as repetition, order and chaos, or moments of contrast, and comment on how they reflect Christopher's perspective, influence the audience or the play's themes.

How to Apply a Structural Technique in an Essay

The structure of the play shapes how the audience receives information and responds emotionally. By examining the sequence of revelations, contrasts between calm and chaos, and the return to familiar patterns at the end, we can see how structure guides the audience throughout the journey, presents the different characters' perspectives and shapes compassion and understanding. When writing about structure, focus on *how* the scenes build meaning and *why* certain moments are revealed or repeated at key points in the play.

Sequential revelations are used effectively control what the audience knows and when. The discovery of Judy's letters, read aloud by Siobhan, gradually uncovers the truth about Christopher's family. This structured delay mirrors detective fiction, sustaining suspense while revealing Christopher's logical, step-by-step approach to understanding events. By postponing Ed's confession until after this discovery, the structure heightens the emotional impact and deepens the audience's sympathy for Christopher. The organisation of these moments ensures that the audience experiences revelation and betrayal at the same pace as he does.

🖊 Quick Recap Task:

List three structural features that are used in the play and explain how each one helps the audience understand Christopher's perspective.

🖊 Reflection Prompt:

Which moment in the play had the biggest structural impact on you as a reader or viewer and why ?

AO2 Starter Pack – Good Techniques to Learn First

These techniques appear frequently in the play and are straightforward to apply. Try to use at least one from each category when writing about a character, theme, or moment in the play.

- **Language:** Literalism, symbolism, repetition
- **Form:** Framing device, projection, ensemble movement
- **Structure:** Sequential revelations, motif, cyclical ending

Try to use **one from each group** in your writing.

Other Key Phrases for AO2 Analysis

These sentence starters can also help you write fluent, precise AO2 commentary on how techniques create effect.

- *The [word / phrase / image] "[quote]" suggests...*
- *This moment increases tension because...*
- *The structure of the scene highlights / reinforces...*
- *The audience is positioned to understand / feel...*
- *The contrast between [X] and [Y] reveals...*
- *This technique helps to show how...*

Self-test: Language, Form and Structure

Multiple Choice Questions:

Choose the most accurate answer for each question:

1. Christopher's line *"The dog is dead"* is an example of:
   a. Symbolism
   b. Metaphor
   c. Literalism
   d. Emotive language
2. Why are projections and multimedia used on stage?
   a. To make the set more realistic
   b. To display Christopher's inner thoughts visually
   c. To distract the audience from dialogue
   d. To represent other characters' emotions
3. When Christopher asks *"Does that mean I can do anything?"* the moment reflects:
   a. His complete confidence and certainty
   b. His uncertainty and need for reassurance
   c. His disappointment with the exam
   d. His confusion about Siobhan's role

Short Answer Tasks (write 2-3 sentences for each)

4. Give one example of **emotive language** in the play and explain its effect on the audience.
5. How are **lighting or sound** used to represent Christopher's feelings?

The Curious Incident of the Dog in the Night-time

Explain & Explore

Write one developed paragraph for each question:

6. How does Siobhan's narration shape the audience's understanding of Christopher's thoughts and emotions?
7. Why does the play combine realistic dialogue with stylised movement and projection?

Chapter 8
How to write your essays

Using a Structure to Plan and Write Effective Essays

In Section A of Edexcel IGCSE English Literature Paper 2, you are required to write one 30-mark essay. Your response must demonstrate close understanding of the text (AO1) and a clear analysis of the writer uses language, form and structure to create meaning (AO2). This chapter provides a structured approach to answering exam-style questions, helping you progress from initial planning to analytical writing through a three-step process.

Step 1: Understand the Question

Start by identifying what the question asks you to explore. Most questions will focus on:

- A specific character (e.g. Christopher, Ed, Judy)
- A particular theme (e.g. truth, family, independence)
- A technique (e.g. structure, staging, narration)

The Curious Incident of the Dog in the Night-time

Ask:

- What is the question really asking me to explore?
- What does the audience need to know or feel?
- Which techniques (language, form, structure) reveal it most clearly?

Step 2: Select Quotations

Choose three to five quotations from across the play that:

- Clearly relate to the focus of the question
- Offer opportunities to explore language, structure, or dramatic technique
- Reflect character development or thematic significance

Quotations should be concise and specific. Long passages are rarely needed. Remember: stage directions, projections, and moments of silence can also be used as "evidence" in your analysis as the play is highly visual and physical.

Step 3: Plan and Write Using PEEL or PETAL

Writing analytical paragraphs is a key part of responding to essay questions in Edexcel IGCSE English Literature. You should aim to write **three to four well-developed paragraphs** in your 30-mark essay.

There are two structures you can use, depending on your confidence and level of analysis:

Step 3A: PEEL (For Developing Writers)

The PEEL structure is ideal if you are building confidence with essay writing. It focuses on making a clear point, supporting it with evidence, and explaining its meaning in relation to the question.

Point - Make a clear statement that answers the question.

Evidence - Support your point with a relevant quote.

Explanation - Explain what the quote shows/represents about the character or theme.

Link - Connect back to the question or Priestley's purpose.

Worked Example Using PEEL

Question

How does the play present the relationship between Christopher and his father?

Sample Paragraph (Step 3A – PEEL):

Ed is presented as a caring but frustrated father. When he admits, "I was in a bad way," it reflects his realisation and guilt after losing control. This suggests that although Ed loves Christopher deeply, he struggles to express his emotions clearly and calmly. This tension highlights the difficulties of parenting and communication, helping the audience understand and empathise with both characters.

The Curious Incident of the Dog in the Night-time

PEEL Sentence Starters

P: The play presents [character/theme] as…

E: This is shown when [character/action/stage direction] …

E: This suggests that…

L: This reinforces the play's exploration of [idea, e.g. family, trust, independence].

Final Tip for Practice

Use PEEL when you're getting started with essay writing, especially if you're working on:

- Structuring clear points
- Building confidence in using quotations
- Practising linking ideas back to the theme or question

As you improve, aim to include **technique identification** and **deeper analysis**, which you can do by transitioning to PETAL.

Step 3B: PETAL (For Higher-Level Analysis)

The **PETAL** Paragraph Structure

Point - Make a clear statement in response to the question.

Evidence - Provide a relevant quote from the text.

Technique - Identify a literary or dramatic technique used.

Analysis - Explain how the technique creates meaning or affects the audience.

Link - Connect back to the question or explain Priestley's broader purpose.

Worked Example Using PETAL

Question:

How is Christopher's independence presented in the play?

Planning Notes (Step 1):

- Central theme: independence and courage
- Development: from dependence at home to self-reliant action in London
- Techniques: direct speech (declarative statements), stagecraft (projection, sound, movement), structure (real-time sequence)

Quotation Bank (Step 2):

- "If he killed Wellington, he could kill me too."
- "Does that mean I can do anything?"
- Staging of the train station sequence — projection, lighting, and ensemble movement showing confusion and determination

Sample Paragraph (Step 3 – PETAL):

Christopher's growing independence is represented most clearly in his journey to London to find his mother after Ed confesses to killing Wellington. Christopher becomes more afraid of Ed than of the uncertain journey, as he believes because *"(Ed) killed Wellington. That means he could kill me, too."* Lighting and ensemble movement recreate the confusion of the station, helping the audience to sense how overwhelming the journey is for him. Judy's shock at seeing him alone reinforces how far he has come in self-reliance, showing that his independence has been hard-won through courage and determination.

PETAL Sentence Starters

You may find these sentence frames helpful when planning:

- **Point**: The play presents [character/theme] as...
- **Evidence**: This is shown when [quote]...
- **Technique**: The use of [technique] suggests...
- **Analysis**: This implies... / This highlights... / This allows the audience to see.../This creates an effect of
- **Link**: This supports the play's message about... / It reinforces the theme of...

Final Tip for Practice

Aim to write three to four PETAL paragraphs in a 30-mark essay. Each paragraph should focus on a single idea, support it with precise evidence, and build towards a coherent overall argument.

Sample Essay Plans

Before writing a full essay, it is important to create a plan that structures your response clearly and logically. A strong essay plan helps ensure:

- You stay focused on the question
- Each paragraph supports and builds your argument
- That you to balance your discussion of characters, themes and techniques
- You cover the play's key moments

This section provides two model plans for commonly asked themes and character questions. Each plan outlines three key paragraphs, showing how to build a thoughtful and exam-ready response.

Example Plan: Theme-Based Question

Question:

How is the theme of honesty and communication explored in The Curious Incident of the Dog in the Night-time?

You must consider language, form and structure in your answer.

Introduction

Define the theme briefly.

Explain that honesty is essential but often difficult to maintain. For Christopher, truth provides order and safety, while for others, honesty becomes complicated by emotion and guilt. The play explores how communication, both its success and its failure, shapes trust and connection.

Paragraph 1 – Christopher's literal honesty

- Quote: *"I find people confusing."*
- Technique: Literalism and direct narration
- Analysis: Reveals his difficulty with figurative or emotional language, highlighting why clarity is vital to him.
- Link: Encourages the audience to value his honesty, even when others see it as bluntness or misunderstanding.

Paragraph 2 – Ed's dishonesty and regret

- Quote: *"I'm sorry. I'm sorry. I was in a bad way."*
- Technique: Repetition and emotive language
- Analysis: Exposes his guilt and the breakdown of trust caused by lies. The repeated apology conveys desperation and remorse.
- Link: Suggests that dishonesty, even when meant to protect, leads to emotional harm and isolation.

Paragraph 3 – Siobhan as a model of clear and honest communication

- Quote: *"This is good Christopher."*
- Technique: Supportive tone and reassurance
- Analysis: Siobhan's speech models patience, empathy, and understanding. Her communication creates safety and confidence for Christopher.
- Link: Represents a contrast to the adults' avoidance and honesty as care and guidance.

Conclusion

Summarise how communication defines the relationships in the play.

Honesty brings pain and conflict, but also growth and understanding. The characters show that trust depends on openness and that communication, even when imperfect, holds people together.

Example Plan – Character-Based Question

Question:

How is Ed shown to be both flawed and caring in the play?

Introduction

Ed is a complex father figure who struggles with honesty but has deep love for Christopher. Mention that despite his parental role, he is presented as vulnerable, capable of both mistakes and growth.

Paragraph 1 – Ed's protective nature

- Quote: "I cooked his meals. I cleaned his clothes."
- Technique: Simple declarative sentences; repetition.
- Analysis: Emphasises Ed's consistency and care through everyday actions. His language lists routine tasks rather than emotions, showing that for him, love is expressed through responsibility and persistence.
- Link: Highlights how parental love in the play is shown through action rather than expression.

Paragraph 2 – Ed's flawed choices and dishonesty

- Quote: *"I killed Wellington."*
- Technique: Understatement; abrupt syntax
- Analysis: The simplicity of the confession intensifies its impact. This moment exposes how Ed's lies and impulsive actions destroy Christopher's trust. The act feels desperate, not malicious, revealing how pressure and grief distort judgment.

- Link: Suggests that love and failure coexist, and that emotional strain can lead to destructive choices.

Paragraph 3 – Ed's Guilt and Reconciliation

- Quote: *"I'm sorry. I'm sorry. I was in a bad way."*
- Technique: Repetition; emotive apology
- Analysis: The repetition conveys sincerity and regret. Ed's speech emphasises his struggle for forgiveness. His apology becomes an act of vulnerability, showing that honesty can begin to rebuild connection.
- Link: Reinforces one of the play's key ideas — that reconciliation depends on openness and patience.

Conclusion

Summarise Ed's nature as both caring and flawed. In the play, his character explores parental imperfection and the burden of responsibility. Through Ed, the audience sees the challenges of loving someone whose world works differently from your own, and the importance of to acknowledging mistakes and working to repair broken relationships.

Skeleton Structures for Essay Responses

A skeleton essay structure provides a clear blueprint for writing analytical responses. It ensures your essay stays focused, covers Assessment Objectives (AO1 and AO2), and flows logically from introduction to conclusion. Use these templates as a starting point for any theme or character question.

Essay Skeleton: General Format

1. Introduction

Set the focus of your essay and define the theme or character. Mention the play's purpose and overall message.

Template:

In *The Curious Incident of the Dog in the Night-time*, the theme of [insert theme] is explored through [insert character(s)/event(s)]. The play invites the audience to experience the world through Christopher's perspective and to reflect on [insert idea]. This essay will examine how [language/form/structure] is used to present [theme or character].

2. Body Paragraphs (3-4 PETAL paragraphs)

Each paragraph should:

- Introduce one clear idea
- Use a short quotation or stage direction as evidence
- Identify a technique (language, form or structure)
- Analyse the effect on the audience
- Link back to the play's purpose or message

Paragraph Starter Template (PETAL):

- **Point**: In the play, [character/theme] is presented as...
- **Evidence**: This is shown when [quote]...
- **Technique**: The use of [technique] suggests...
- **Analysis**: This highlights... / This helps the audience understand... / This creates the impression that...
- **Link**: This reinforces the play's message about...

When developing your paragraphs, aim to cover a range of ideas. For example:

- A character who changes or grows (e.g. Christopher)
- A key relationship or source of conflict (e.g. Ed and Judy, or Christopher and Siobhan)
- A structural or theatrical device (e.g. narration, projection, soundscape)

3. Conclusion

Return to the question and summarise how the play uses language, form or structure to explore the human experience and perspective.

Example:

In conclusion, [character/device/theme] effectively explores [central idea]. Through Christopher's journey, the play encourages the audience to view and experience the world differently, and with empathy, understanding and curiosity. The ending highlights how [characters/ themes] can [grow together/ be developed], shaped by trust, communication, and personal discovery.

Why Use This Structure

This approach gives you the flexibility to adapt your ideas while ensuring your essay meets the criteria for clear, critical, and focused analysis. It also helps you balance **AO1** (understanding of the play) with **AO2** (analysis of techniques).

Chapter 10 Practice Questions contains a range of sample questions organised by theme. Use these to practise writing essay plans and eventually full essays.

Planning Templates

Effective essays begin with thoughtful planning. This section provides **printable and reusable templates** to help you organise your ideas before you start writing. Planning allows you to:

- Stay focused on the question
- Select relevant evidence and techniques
- Build logical, structured responses
- Ensure each paragraph contributes to your overall argument

These templates can be used for timed practice, homework, or pre-writing exercises in class.

How to Use It

- Start with the **essay question** and work downward.
- Fill in the quotation bank early as this will guide your paragraph ideas.
- Match each point to a character, relationship or event.
- Decide which **technique (language, form or structure)** you'll highlight.
- Use your plan to guide a PETAL or PEEL-based essay.

The Curious Incident of the Dog in the Night-time

Essay Planning Template: Use this structure to map out your response before you write.

Essay Question:

Theme/Focus of Question:

Key Message/Stephens' Purpose:

Quote Bank (3-5 key quotes)

1.

2.

3.

4.

5.

Paragraph 1 – Main Point

Linked Character/Theme/Event

Technique(s) to Include

Paragraph 2 – Main Point

Linked Character/Theme/Event

Technique(s) to Include

Paragraph 3 – Main Point

Linked Character/Theme/Event

Technique(s) to Include

Conclusion – Final Message

How does the play want the audience to reflect or feel by the end?

Chapter 9
Quick Recap Tools

This section provides concise revision tasks to help you consolidate your understanding of *The Curious Incident of the Dog in the Night-time*. The following exercises support retention of key content and are designed to be used independently or as part of classroom review.

Each activity reinforces core areas of the play including key quotes, characters, themes, and structural features while also preparing you for common exam requirements.

Revision Checklist

You should be confident in each of the following areas before the exam. Use this checklist to identify strengths and revision priorities.

Colour My Learning

Area of Knowledge

Understand the play's focus on Christopher's perspective and journey

Identify and explain the play's key themes

Know the role and development of each major character

Recall 3-5 quotations for each theme and character

Recognise use of narration, projection, soundscape, lighting, and ensemble movement.

Analyse how language, form and structure create meaning (AO2)

Apply PETAL structure to write developed paragraphs

Identify key events and explain their dramatic function.

Fill-in-the-Blanks – Key Quotes

Complete the quotations using your knowledge of the play:

1. "Father said you were _____, but he _____." (Speaker: Christopher)
2. "I was not a very _____ _____, Christopher." (Speaker: Judy)
3. "I'm _____. I'm _____. I was in a _____ _____." (Speaker: Ed)
4. "I decided that I was going to do some _____." (Speaker: Christopher)
5. "You're going to have to learn to _____ me." (Speaker: Ed)
6. "I can't tell _____." (Speaker: Christopher)

The Curious Incident of the Dog in the Night-time

Multiple Choice Questions

7. Which theme is most closely linked to Christopher's journey to London?
   a. Social status
   b. Courage
   c. Romantic love
   d. Justice
8. The station scene's overlapping voices and noise are an example of:
   a. Monologue
   b. Symbolism
   c. Soundscape
   d. Exposition
9. The play's framing device is:
   a. A rotating set
   b. Christopher's book read aloud by Siobhan
   c. A voice-over narrator
   d. A prologue by Ed
10. Which staging choice best shows Christopher's thought processes?
    a. Soliloquy
    b. Projection and multimedia
    c. Costume changes
    d. Flashback
11. Which technique does Stephens use to build suspense and gradually reveal truths?
    a. Cliffhanger
    b. Sequential revelations
    c. Foreshadowing
    d. Direct address

12. The play's structure is best described as:
    a. Cyclical
    b. Fragmented and episodic
    c. Linear
    d. Flashback-only
13. Siobhan's role in the play is mainly to:
    a. Cause conflict
    b. Explain Christopher's thoughts to the audience
    c. Hide information
    d. Provide comic relief
14. When Christopher says "It made me feel safe," what theme is highlighted?
    a. Loss and grief
    b. Trust and independence
    c. Class and status
    d. Conflict and anger
15. Which form feature does Frantic Assembly's staging rely on most?
    a. Naturalism
    b. Physical theatre
    c. Realistic props
    d. Still images only
16. What does Christopher's final question, "Does that mean I can do anything?" show?
    a. Complete certainty
    b. Confidence and doubt mixed
    c. Anger towards Siobhan
    d. Denial of change

The Curious Incident of the Dog in the Night-time

Final Writing Practice

Use the PETAL structure to write a paragraph answering:

Question:

How is staging used to present Christopher's experience of chaos in the London Underground scene?

Your paragraph should include:

- A clear point linked to the question
- A relevant quote or stage direction
- A named technique (e.g. soundscape, projection, ensemble movement, lighting)
- Analysis of meaning and effect
- A link back to the play's purpose

If you're not ready yet, don't worry

- Review your **quote banks**
- Revisit **character profiles and themes** in Chapters 3 and 5
- Return to the **essay planning templates** in Chapter 8

Use this guide to help you revise actively, test yourself regularly, and go into your exam prepared and confident.

Chapter 10
Practice Questions

The best way to build confidence in your exam responses is through regular, focused practice. This section gives you a chance to apply everything you've learned, from understanding characters and themes to using language, form, and structure in your writing.

You do not need to write full essays every time. Start by planning your response, choosing relevant quotes, or writing just one strong paragraph. With each step, you'll become more familiar with how exam questions are phrased and how to approach them clearly and calmly.

Use the observed trends below to guide your revision. You will notice that some types of questions come up again and again, and that's a good thing. The more you practise, the more prepared you'll feel.

Observed Trends

Recurring Themes: Ideas of courage, family, and trust are frequent recurring themes

Character Focus: Questions also centre on Christopher, Siobhan Ed, Judy, and Mr and Mrs Shears inviting close analysis of relationships and emotional development.

Thematic Pairings: Exams typically offer a choice between a theme-based question and a character-based question, allowing you to select based on your strengths.

Stage-craft: Occasionally questions focus on the performance of the play, considering how aspects of it relate to the story.

Revision Tips

Thematic Preparation: Organise revision materials by theme to facilitate targeted study sessions.

Quote Integration: Associate key quotations with specific themes to enhance analytical responses.

Practice Essays: Write practice essays for each theme to develop a versatile approach to potential exam questions.

Honesty and Trust

Explore how honesty and trust are presented in *The Curious Incident of the Dog in the Night-time*.
You must consider language, form and structure in your answer.

'Father said you were dead, but he lied.'
How does the play use this moment to explore trust and honesty?
You must consider language, form and structure in your answer.

How is the theme of trust explored through Christopher's relationship with Ed?
You must consider language, form and structure in your answer.

Family, Love, and Care

How are the challenges of family relationships explored in the play?
You must consider language, form and structure in your answer.

Explore how Judy and Ed's behaviour towards Christopher represents both love and failure.
You must consider language, form and structure in your answer.

'Siobhan helps Christopher find calm in a confusing world.'
How does Siobhan represent care and understanding in the play?
You must consider language, form and structure in your answer.

Courage and Independence

'Does that mean I can do anything?'
How is Christopher's growing independence presented?
You must consider language, form and structure in your answer.

How does Christopher's journey to London show his courage and growth?
You must consider language, form and structure in your answer.

Explore how the use of sound and lighting reflects Christopher's emotional state in moments of fear.
You must consider language, form and structure in your answer.

Loss and Grief

How is the theme of loss presented through Wellington's death and its aftermath?
You must consider language, form and structure in your answer.

How is Christopher's narration used to show unconventional expressions of grief?
You must consider language, form and structure in your answer.

'Grief affects everyone differently.'
To what extent is this idea presented through Ed and Judy's relationship?
You must consider language, form and structure in your answer.

Anger and Conflict

'Christopher often experiences conflict between emotion and logic.'
How far do you agree with this view?
You must consider language, form and structure in your answer.

How are dialogue and stagecraft used to convey anger and misunderstanding in the play?
You must consider language, form and structure in your answer.
(Also relevant to Staging)

'Ed's anger is rooted in love.'
How far do you agree with this view?
You must consider language, form and structure in your answer.

Order and Chaos

How are structure and staging used to explore the contrast between order and chaos?
You must consider language, form and structure in your answer.
(Also relevant to Staging)

Explore how mathematical patterns and repetition are used to create order in the play.
You must consider language, form and structure in your answer.

Adventure and Discovery

'Christopher's journey is both physical and emotional.'
How is this dual journey presented?
You must consider language, form and structure in your answer.

How is discovery presented as a source of both anxiety and achievement?
You must consider language, form and structure in your answer.

Dramatic Form and Structure

How is the play-within-a-play structure used to frame Christopher's story?
You must consider language, form and structure in your answer.

Explore how the non-linear structure and narration help the audience see the world through Christopher's eyes.
You must consider language, form and structure in your answer.

How are lighting, sound, and movement used to create shifts in pace and tension?
You must consider language, form and structure in your answer.

Symbolism and Staging

How does the play use visual and physical symbolism to convey key ideas?
You must consider language, form and structure in your answer.

'The stage becomes a map of Christopher's mind.'
How are form and staging used to explore perception and logic?
You must consider language, form and structure in your answer.

Explore how Toby symbolises Christopher's need for comfort and stability.

You must consider language, form and structure in your answer.

Download: *The Curious Incident of the Dog in the Night-time* – Past Exam Questions by Theme (Ebook)

As you have purchased this revision guide, you can download our companion booklet *Past Exam Questions by Theme* free of charge from our publisher's website.

To access your free copy:

1. Visit: **www.bailbrooklane.com**
2. Navigate to The Curious Incident of the Dog in the Night-time Past Year Exam Questions by Theme
3. Click **Add to Basket**
4. On the basket page, enter the coupon code: **CIDNPASTQUES**
5. Click **Apply Coupon** — the price will reduce to £0
6. Proceed to **Checkout**, enter your details, and place your order
7. You will receive an email with a secure download link.

You may download the ebook **up to two times**. If you have any difficulty accessing your copy, please contact: **info@bailbrooklane.com**

Chapter 11
Further Reading and Resources

While this guide offers a complete, exam-focused approach to *The Curious Incident of the Dog in the Night-time*, exploring wider resources can deepen understanding and sharpen analytical skills. Engaging with diverse materials helps you appreciate how different critics, directors, and audiences interpret the play, and how Stephens' theatrical choices connect to wider contexts. Exploring additional resources allows you to:

- Discover how others interpret characters, structure, and themes.
- Explore the social, cultural, and theatrical background of the play.
- Familiarise yourself with how examiners mark and assess real student responses
- Access interactive and alternative formats (e.g. videos, articles, podcasts) to suit your preferred learning styles

The following curated list includes high-quality websites, examiner materials, and revision platforms that extend beyond the basics. They are particularly useful for:

- High-achieving students aiming to stretch their analysis.
- Teachers seeking enrichment or discussion materials.
- Learners who want to approach essays with greater independence and confidence.

Use these resources selectively and critically. Not all interpretations will align exactly with Edexcel's assessment criteria, but engaging with different viewpoints will strengthen your ability to form your own supported arguments.

ColourMyLearning

colourmylearning.com

For printable worksheets, revision summaries, and topic-by-topic blog posts, ColourMyLearning provides free, accessible content designed to complement this guide. Whether you're revising a theme, exploring character development, or practising PEEL writing, these articles reinforce your understanding and link directly to key exam skills.

New posts are added regularly to align with the Edexcel IGCSE and GCSE English Literature curriculum.

BBC Bitesize – The Curious Incident of the Dog in the Night-time (play)

bbc.co.uk/bitesize

BBC Bitesize offers concise, reliable summaries of key characters, themes, and techniques for *The Curious Incident of the Dog in the Night-time*. Its visual layouts and quizzes make it especially useful for quick revision and consolidating understanding. While tailored for general GCSE, it complements the Edexcel IGCSE course effectively for foundational knowledge.

Edexcel Examiner Reports – English Literature Paper 2

qualifications.pearson.com

These official documents provide direct insight into how students are assessed in real exam conditions. Each report includes commentary on past responses, common mistakes, and advice from examiners. Essential reading for students aiming to refine their exam technique and understand how marks are awarded under AO1 and AO2.

Theatre and Production Insights

National Theatre Education – Frantic Assembly Workshops

www.nationaltheatre.org.uk/learning

Behind-the-scenes insight into how physical theatre and projection were used to stage Christopher's perspective.

Frantic Assembly Resource Pack

https://www.franticassembly.co.uk/resources/the-curious-incident-of-the-dog-in-the-night-time-resource-pack

Includes director's notes, production photographs, and rehearsal exercises exploring the adaptation process.

Interviews with Simon Stephens

https://www.nationaltheatre.org.uk/learn-explore/schools/teacher-resources/adapting-curious-incident/

Available via the *National Theatre YouTube channel*. These offer valuable insight into his writing aims, adaptation choices, and views on representing neurodiversity.

Contextual and Analytical Reading

Mark Haddon, *The Curious Incident of the Dog in the Night-time* (2003 novel)

Reading the original novel will help you compare Stephens' adaptation techniques and understand how a narrative can be transformed into its theatrical form.

Articles on Neurodiversity and Representation in Theatre

You can enrich your contextual understanding by exploring essays on inclusion, empathy, and the staging of neurodiverse experiences.

Answer Key

Chapter 2 Story Overview

End of Chapter Self-test

Multiple Choice Questions

1. b) In Mrs Shears's garden
2. c) He hits a policeman who touches him
3. a) Mrs Alexander
4. c) A box of letters from Judy

Short Answer (sample answers)

5. Ed tells Christopher that Judy is dead because he wants to protect Christopher from the truth that she left home with Roger Shears and also because he is angry and frustrated that she has left him. Christopher discovers the truth when he finds a hidden box of letters from Judy.

6. Christopher decides to leave Swindon and travel alone to London to find his mother. This is significant because it shows his bravery and independence, as he leaves behind his routines and faces his fears.
7. The play ends with Christopher reflecting on his achievements. He asks, "Does that mean I can do anything?", leaving the audience with hope about his future.

Longer Task (sample answers)

- **Part 1:** Christopher grows through his detective work. At first, he is focused on solving Wellington's murder, but his investigation reveals bigger family secrets. By the end of Part 1, he has lost trust in Ed and shown determination to make his own decisions and choices.
- **Part 2:** Christopher's growth is shown in his bravery and independence. He travels to London alone, finds Judy, excels at his Maths exam, and begins to imagine a future for himself. Although his family is still divided, he proves he can achieve difficult goals.

Chapter 3 Main Characters

End of Chapter Self-test

Multiple Choice:

1. c. Mrs Alexander
2. d. All of the above
3. b. She feels guilty and wants to explain herself.
4. b. Siobhan

5. b. It begins Christopher's investigation

Short Answer (sample answers)

6. Christopher explains that honesty is one of his core values. It highlights the contrast between his straightforward nature and the dishonesty of the adults around him.
7. Ed's lies about Judy damage his relationship with Christopher. Discovering the hidden letters and learning that Ed killed Wellington makes Christopher lose trust in his father and pushes him to leave home.
8. Judy admits her guilt and inadequacy as a parent. The plain, confessional tone asserts her view that she is a flawed parent.
9. Siobhan reads from Christopher's book and explains his thoughts. This allows the audience to understand his perspective more clearly and with empathy.

Longer Tasks – Model Answer Outlines

Character & Theme Connection – Family and Relationships

Example answer:

10. Christopher
    - Christopher character is used to explore challenges, strain and love within a family. He loves his parents but struggles with trusting them after they have lied to him.
    - Quotation: *"I always tell the truth."* This contrasts with Ed's secrecy and Judy's absence, which complicate family bonds.

- Christopher's book is staged as a play, allowing the audience experience his family relationships from his immediate perspective.

Other approaches:

- Ed symbolises protective love but damaged trust.
- Judy's love is mixed with guilt, highlighting parental imperfection.

Compare & Contrast

Example answer:

11. Judy and Ed
    - Ed is protective but lies to Christopher, losing his trust. Judy is more emotionally available but left him, which is inconsistent with her expected role as a mother.
    - When Ed says *"It's bloody hard telling the truth all the time."* he admits to telling lies need for control. Judy's line *"I was not a very good mother, Christopher"* reveals her honesty and regret.
    - Christopher's completely loses trust in Ed when he admits to hiding Judy's letters and to killing Wellington. This catalyses Christopher's need to see his mother, and his bond with Judy grows again. Both parents are flawed characters although develop emotionally through the play.

The Curious Incident of the Dog in the Night-time

Character Symbolism

Example answer:

12. Wellington
    - Wellington's death begins the story and sets up Christopher's detective investigation. It provides the structure of the play and drives him to search for truth.
    - The killing symbolises secrecy, anger, and mistrust. Ed's violent action reflects the hidden tensions within the Boone family.
    - Opening the play with this shocking image, shapes how the audience sees Christopher's struggles and perspective: his search for truth starts with violence close to home.

Supporting Characters – Mrs Alexander, Mrs Shears, or Roger Shears

Example answer (Mrs Alexander):

- She is kind to Christopher, offering to be truthful to him.
- Her honesty about Judy's affair links to the theme of truth.
- Her role matters because she is one of the few adults outside the family who supports Christopher.

Example answer (Mrs Shears):

- She is hostile when Wellington is found: *"What the hell were you doing in my garden?"*
- Her reaction sets the story in motion and represents mistrust in the community.
- Her presence highlights how some neighbours fail to provide support.

Example answer (Roger Shears):

- He is unreliable and emotionally distant, as Judy explains in her letters.
- He symbolises betrayal and the instability of adult relationships.
- His absence from the stage underlines his lack of responsibility.

Chapter 4 Context

End of Chapter Self-test

Multiple Choice:

1. b) Simon Stephens
2. b) Siobhan
3. b) Frantic Assembly

The Curious Incident of the Dog in the Night-time

Short Answer (sample answers)

4. The play highlights both the misunderstandings surrounding autism and the need for inclusive education. Christopher's logical approach and difficulties with metaphor reflect wider conversations in early 2000s Britain about supporting neurodiverse students.
5. Siobhan acts as a bridge between Christopher and the audience. Her calm, supportive voice makes his story clearer and more accessible, while also reflecting good inclusive teaching practice.
6. Judy and Ed's separation reflects the rising divorce rates of the early 2000s. The play represents the strain of family breakdown, but also explores how parents and children can rebuild trust after separation.

Context-Based Tasks (Sample Responses)

7. The grid-like stage design mirrors Christopher's logical mind. Projections and sound effects show sensory overload, helping the audience understand how overwhelming the world can feel for him. Ensemble movement creates visual metaphors, such as the "space" scene, allowing us to experience his imagination.
8. Many would see this as both inspiring and brave, reflecting growing awareness of disability rights and independence. Some might also recognise the fear and anxiety his parents feel, reflecting wider social

debates about how much freedom to allow children with additional needs.

Chapter 5 Main Themes

End of Chapter Self-test

Multiple Choice:

1. b. Loss and Grief
2. c. Siobhan
3. b. Ed reveals the truth about Wellington
4. a. Courage and independence
5. a. "I decided that I was going to do some detecting."
6. b. Order and Chaos

Short Answer (sample answers)

7. Siobhan helps Christopher interpret metaphors and express himself clearly. She represents supportive communication and exemplifies how gentle and understanding language builds trust.
8. The train station uses sound and ensemble movement to overwhelm the stage. Christopher's need to block out noise and find order reflects the struggle between control and chaos.
9. Judy says, *"I'm sorry, Christopher. I never meant to hurt you."* This connects to the theme of loss and grief, showing her regret and desire to rebuild a relationship. The audience sees an attempt at reconciliation.

The Curious Incident of the Dog in the Night-time

Longer Tasks – Sample Responses

10. Paragraph: how the theme of trust changes throughout the play

At the start of the play, Christopher trusts his father completely, depending on him for care and protection. This trust is destroyed when Christopher discovers Judy's letters and realises that Ed lied about his mother's death and about Wellington's murder. The line *"Father said you were dead. But he lied"* captures both the shock of betrayal and the collapse of security Christopher had taken for granted. By the end of the play, some trust is rebuilt, but Christopher has learnt to rely more on his own independence, showing that trust can change and evolve rather than be fully restored.

11. Theme Paragraphs (sample answers)

Family and Relationships

Christopher's relationship with Ed reflects the theme of family as both protective and fragile. Ed cares for Christopher practically, reminding him, *"I cooked his meals. I cleaned his clothes. I looked after him."* However, his dishonesty about Judy damages their bond. . Their relationship shows how love within families is complicated and can be tested by mistakes and secrets.

Courage and Independence

Christopher is courageous when he decides to travel alone to London, even though the journey overwhelms him. The staging of the train station, with its noise and movement, highlights the fear he faces. His final line, *"Does that mean I can do anything?"* reflects the courage he has built through persistence. The play presents courage as a gradual achievement, gained by confronting fear step-by-step.

Love, Care, and Attachment

Judy's apology to Christopher reflects the theme of love through regret and repair. When she says, *"I'm sorry, Christopher. I never meant to hurt you,"* she tries to rebuild the bond that was damaged by her absence. Love is expressed through actions and reconciliation rather than declarations, showing how care can continue even after mistakes.

Anger and Conflict

Ed's temper reflects the theme of anger and conflict most directly. When Ed swears *"Don't give me that bollocks. You knew exactly what you were bloody doing."* His use of expletives and angry tone conveys his frustration and anger. When he hits Christopher out of anger, it further damages their relationship and forces Ed to apologise repeatedly. The play presents anger as a destructive force that stems from stress and grief, showing how conflict strains relationships but can also lead to reflection and change.

Chapter 6 Glossary of Literary and Dramatic Terms

End of Chapter Self-test

Multiple Choice:

1. b. Literalism
2. b. Framing device
3. c. Prime numbers

Short Answer (sample answers)

4. Narration is when Siobhan reads from Christophers book, addressing the audience directly to explain or frame events. Dialogue is the conversation between characters on stage.
5. An example of symbolism is Toby the rat, which represents comfort and security for Christopher.
6. Ensemble movement presents Christopher's perspective by turning abstract experiences into physical action. For example, actors carrying him to show him "floating in space" or surrounding him to stage the chaos of the train station.

Fill in the Blanks

7. A <u>motif</u> is a repeated image or phrase that helps reinforce a theme.
8. The term **direct address** refers to a moment when Christopher or Siobhan speak directly to the audience.

9. Projection is used to show Christopher's <u>thoughts</u> on stage.

Reflection Prompt *(Example Response)*

10. Projection, soundscape, and motif help me explain how the play presents Christopher's world. I use them to show how his thoughts are made visible, how overwhelming environments are staged, and how recurring patterns reinforce his need for order.

Chapter 7 Language Form and Structure

End of Chapter Self-test

Multiple Choice:

1. c. Literalism
2. b. Sequential revelations
3. b. His uncertainty and need for reassurance

Short Answer (sample answers)

4. An example of **emotive language** is Judy's line, *"I never meant to hurt you."* The apology asks for sympathy yet also implies her guilt and regret. It helps the audience understand the pain caused by her absence and dishonesty.
5. Stephens uses **lighting and sound** to show Christopher's emotions. Harsh, bright lights and loud overlapping sounds reflect moments of fear or overload, while softer light and calm tones appear in

safe, reassuring moments with Siobhan. This helps the audience feel what Christopher experiences.

Explain & Explore (example answers):

6. Siobhan's narration provides clarity and balance to the play. As she reads from Christopher's book, her calm voice and measured tone contrast with the chaos on stage, helping the audience interpret what Christopher cannot explain himself. She guides the audience through complex emotions and events, translating Christopher's logical observations into emotional understanding. Siobhan as both narrator and mentor, ensures that Christopher's world is accessible and sympathetic to the audience.
7. Realistic speech is combined with stylised movement to present both the outer and inner worlds of the play. The dialogue keeps the story grounded in family conflict and emotion, while projections, choreography, and soundscapes show how Christopher experiences the world through patterns and sensory detail. This contrast allows the audience to see the difference between how events appear and how they feel to Christopher. The combination makes the play more immersive, using theatrical form to mirror the logic and imagination of his mind.

Chapter 9 Quick Recap Tools

Fill-in-the-Blanks – Key Quotes

1. "Father said you were <u>dead</u>, but he <u>lied</u>."
2. "I was not a very <u>good mother</u>, Christopher."
3. "I'm <u>sorry</u>. I'm <u>sorry</u>. I was in a <u>bad way</u>."
4. "I decided that I was going to do some <u>detecting</u>."
5. "You have to learn to <u>trust</u> me."
6. ""I can't tell <u>lies</u>." (Speaker: Christopher)

Multiple Choice Questions

7. b. Courage
8. c. Soundscape
9. b. Christopher's book read aloud by Siobhan
10. b. Projection and multimedia
11. b. Sequential revelations
12. b. Fragmented and episodic
13. b. Explain Christopher's thoughts to the audience
14. b. Trust and independence
15. b. Physical theatre
16. b. Confidence and doubt mixed

The Curious Incident of the Dog in the Night-time

Final Writing Practice – Sample PETAL Paragraph

Sample Answer:

Christopher's experience of chaos is presented well through sound and movement. In the station scene, a **soundscape** of voices and train noises builds intensity while the **ensemble** crowds and lifts Christopher, creating the effect of sensory overload. The **lighting** flashes as the noise peaks, mirroring his confusion but also his determination to keep going. In this moment, the audience experiences Christopher's courage and understand how order can emerge through focus, logic, and persistence.

Acknowledgments

Thank you to the students, teachers, and tutors who have inspired the development of this guide, especially those who ask thoughtful questions, think deeply about the text, and remind us that good literature invites reflection as well as analysis.

Special thanks to everyone who helped review and refine this material, ensuring that it remains both rigorous and accessible. Your feedback has made this guide clearer, stronger, and more useful to students preparing for real exams under real pressure.

Finally, to every reader working through these pages, whether you're revising late at night, learning in class, or quietly building confidence in your own time, thank you. This guide was written for you.

Also by Colour My Learning

Looking for revision guides for other texts?

Explore our full collection of study resources, including upcoming titles, past paper questions, and blog support, at:

www.colourmylearning.com/revision

Whether you're studying *Macbeth*, *Of Mice and Men*, *Jekyll & Hyde*, or poetry, you'll find updates, free materials, and downloadable tools to help you prepare.

Stay up to date and check what's new. We're constantly adding more.

www.ingramcontent.com/pod-product-compliance
Lightning Source LLC
Chambersburg PA
CBHW052034070526
44584CB00016B/2037